ACPL ITE... P9-EDI-427

DISCARDED

3 1833 00271 3268

DEC 30 '68

BUT THAT
I CAN'T BELIEVE!

JOHN
A. T. ROBINSON

BISHOP OF
WOOLWICH

PERSPECTIVES
IN HUMANISM
Planned and Edited by
RUTH NANDA ANSHEN

Board of Editors

W. H. Auden
Richard Courant
Martin C. D'Arcy, S.J.
Theodosius Dobzhansky
Erich Fromm
Werner Heisenberg
Fred Hoyle
Muhammad Zafrulla Khan
Konrad Lorenz
R. M. MacIver
Joseph Needham
I. I. Rabi
Sarvepalli Radhakrishnan
Karl Rahner, S.J.
Harold Rosenberg
Alexander Sachs
James Johnson Sweeney
Yoshinori Takeuchi

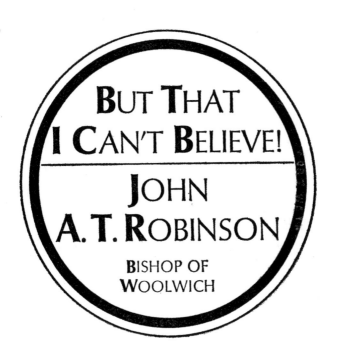

But That I Can't Believe!

John A. T. Robinson

Bishop of Woolwich

THE NEW AMERICAN LIBRARY

"Perspectives in Humanism: The Future of
Tradition," Copyright © 1967 by Ruth Nanda Anshen

Copyright © 1967 by J. A. T. Robinson, Bishop of Woolwich
All rights reserved. No part of this book may be reproduced
without written permission from the publishers.
First Printing

Library of Congress Catalog Card Number: 67-24793
Published by The New American Library, Inc.
1301 Avenue of the Americas, New York, New York 10019
Printed in the United States of America

CONTENTS

1463714

PERSPECTIVES IN HUMANISM
THE FUTURE OF TRADITION
RUTH NANDA ANSHEN

Perspectives in Humanism is designed to affirm that the world, the universe, and man are remarkably stable, elementally unchanging. Protons remain protons, and the other known elements are themselves, even when their atoms are broken; and man remains, in his essence, man. Every form of nature possesses what Aristotle called its own law. The blade of grass does not exist to feed the cow; the cow does not exist in order to give milk to man; and man does not exist to be subdivided, for to subdivide him is to execute him. Man is an organism, a whole, in which segregation of any sort is artificial and in which every phenomenon is a manifestation of the whole. The lawfulness of nature, including man's nature, is a miracle defying understanding.

My Introduction to this Series is not of course to be construed as a prefatory essay for each individual book. These few pages simply attempt to set forth the general aim and purpose of the Series as a whole. They try to point to the humanistic significance of the respective disciplines as represented by those scholars who have been invited to participate in this endeavor.

Perspectives in Humanism submits that there is a

constant process of continuity within the process of change. This process lies in the very nature of man. We ask ourselves: What is this constant? What is it that endures and is the foundation of our intellectual and moral civilization? What is it that we are able to call our humanistic tradition? What is it that must survive and be transmitted to the future if man is to remain human?

The answer is that this constant lies in recognizing what is changeless in the midst of change. It is that heritage of timeless and immutable values on which we can fix our gaze whenever the language of change and decline which history speaks seems to become too overwhelming for the human heart. It offers us the spectacle of the constancy of certain basic forms and ideas throughout a process of continuous social mutations, intellectual development, and scientific revolution. The constant is the original form maintaining itself by transformation and adapting itself to changing social conditions, the continuity which is the very medium of change.

It is the loss of awareness of this constant in our time, not through the failure but rather through the very success of our modern scientific and technological achievements that has produced a society in which it becomes increasingly difficult to live a life that is human.

Perspectives in Humanism tries to confront, and, if possible, show the way to the resolution of, the major dilemma of our epoch: the greatest affliction of the modern mind. This dilemma is created by the magnificent fruits of the industrial revolution on the one hand and by an inexorable technology on the other. It is the acceptance of power as a source of authority and as a substitute for truth and knowledge. It is the dilemma born out of a skepticism in values and a faith in the perfectibility of the mind. It accepts the results of scientific inquiry as carrying self-evident implications, an obvious error. And finally it defines knowledge as a product, accepting lines of force emptied of lines of will, rather than, as indeed it is, a process.

The authors in this Series attempt to show the failure of what has been called scientific humanism, to show the limitation of scientific method which determines only sequences of events without meaning and among these events none more meaningless than man. For modern science is not concerned with human experience, nor with human purposes, and its knowledge of ascertained natural facts can never represent the whole of human nature. Now man is crying out for the recognition of insights derived from other sources, from the awareness that the problem of mechanism and teleology is a legitimate problem, requiring a humanistic solution.

It has always been on the basis of the hypothesis that the world and man's place in it can be understood by reason that the world and man become intelligible. And in all the crises of the mind and heart it has been the belief in the possibility of a solution that has made a solution possible.

Studies of man are made in all institutions of research and higher learning. There is hardly a section of the total scholarly enterprise which does not contribute directly or indirectly to our knowledge of man's nature. Not only philosophy and theology, not only history and the other humanities, not only psychology, sociology, biology, and medicine investigate man's nature and existence, but also the natural sciences do so, at least indirectly, and even directly, whenever they reflect upon their own methods, limits, and purposes.

It is in the light of such considerations that *Perspectives in Humanism* endeavors to show the false antinomy between the scientist and the humanist and the Cartesian error of dualizing mind and body. This Series tries to point to the incoherence of our time which implies the breakdown of integrative relationships, and to demonstrate that in science, as in all other fields of human thought and action, humanism may be preserved only through channels of shared experience and through mutual hopes. Indeed, humanism in these volumes is defined as that force which may render science once more part of universal human discourse. In this, it is here proposed, lies the future of tradition. Our search is for the "ought" which does not derive from facts alone.

In many realms of scholarly work there is an awareness of the fragmentation of man. And there is an increasing recognition that the study of man-made and natural ecological systems is as necessary as the study of isolated particles and elementary reactions. Most impressive has been the reaction of many scientists to the problems of the "atomic age" created by the technical application of their own theories. They realize that the question of the human meaning of scientific research cannot be repressed any longer in view of the immensity of these problems.

In biology and medicine the qualitative uniqueness of every life process, and especially the uniqueness of that process which is called human, has come into the foreground of investigation. And, above all, biology, psychology, and medicine have made parallel efforts to overcome the accepted but untenable split between the psychological and the physiological aspects of human nature, remembering with Aristotle that the soul is the meaning of the body.

Historical studies in all directions, including political, social, economic, cultural, and religious history, have begun to ask the question: What are the characteristics of man as they are manifested in history? The exclusively factual and causal approach to history generally, and its special divisions such as history of the arts, of literature, of societal forms, of religion, has been broken down in many places. The question of meaning has not replaced the question of fact but has given research another dimension and a direct relevance for man's self-interpretation.

This is the situation. No convincing picture of man has arisen in spite of the many ways in which human thought has tried to reach it. But one thing has been achieved: The problem has made itself felt with great force in many places in spite of considerable resistance. This alone would justify a concentrated attempt to seek for preliminary answers and new questions resulting from them. And this is the aim of *Perspectives in Humanism*.

There is, however, another rather serious reason for cooperation in the study of this new and enlarged meaning of humanism. It is the fact that, under the impact of these developments, a linguistic confusion in all important matters of man's existence has taken place in the Western world—a confusion which makes cooperation extremely difficult. Most concepts used in scholarly attempts to draw a picture of man are ambiguous, or obsolete, or fashionable clichés. It is impossible *not* to use them, but they mislead if they are used. This is not a recent development—although the methods of contemporary publicity have supported it and are one of the greatest impediments to healing it—but it is a result of the intellectual and social history of the last centuries. A change is possible only if this history in all its ramifications is studied from the point of view of the disintegration of the language concerning man which has taken place in the last centuries. Such a dialogue is formidable and must be done in terms of a continuous exchange between representatives of the different spheres of knowledge and of cultures. It is our hope that this Series will provide favorable conditions for such an exchange.

The historical approach must be done in interdependence with a systematic approach. Concepts developed in one sphere must show their relevance for other spheres. This also is being done in a casual way in contemporary literature. It must be done methodologically. The departmental boundaries must be trespassed continuously. It is ultimately impossible to make a true statement about the physiological dynamics of the human body without taking into consideration the spirit which forms the flesh. It is ultimately impossible to describe the self-destructive tendencies in a neurotic person without describing the structures of estrangement in man's social existence. These examples can be increased indefinitely. They show that the departmentalization of our knowledge of man, although it was and is a matter of expediency, is at the same time a cause for distortion. Here lies the main positive task of *Perspectives in Humanism*.

Humanism is the ideal pattern supposed to reveal the true nature of man and the task for which he was born — the task of shaping himself into a true man and thereby creating a society worthy of him to be transmitted to future generations. For humanism is a lasting truth, not merely a transitory historical phenomenon. Like the changeless *logos* of which Heraclitus spoke, it pervades the whole process of eternal flux, and may even be said to be like a divine fire that works in each of us whether we know it or not. There stands behind our Western tradition, just as behind the great traditions of the East, a common metaphysical faith which transcends all schisms and conflicts within it.

And just as humanism means that there exists a common humanity beyond all divisiveness, so humanism also means that a unitary nature unites scientist and humanist alike. It can no longer be said that man is either a scientist or a humanist. The knower and the known, the doubter and the doubt, are one. To identify the scientist with a single method, the scientific one, that is, with a single procedure, is a distortion of science. All the powers of the mind, of intuition, of observation (to which the observer brings his own perception), of discursive and nondiscursive knowledge, are brought into play in the achievement of scientific interpretation. And the pre-analytic data of science, if called "facts," are in reality but problematic facts. The only facts initially given for exploration are the facts of humanistic relevance, facts laden or saturated with loose or crude interpretations and demanding therefore reinterpretations by procedures free from what Bacon described as idols of the mind.

The difference between humanistic and scientific meaning is a difference not of kind but of degree. Can it be seriously maintained that, prior to the advent of scientific knowledge, with its elaborate hypotheses and theories, all intent upon the search for the nature of things, men were acquainted merely with sense data, or meaningless impressions? Prescientific knowledge is also knowledge, involving in incipient or inchoate form most of the activities in which science is engaged, such as naming and classifying, numbering and measuring, describing and explaining. And all these aspects are but the humanistic yearning in man's nature to establish a legitimate place for himself in the cosmic scheme from which he feels that he has been estranged. However farflung its hypotheses or comprehensive its theories, science has no objects for its application save such as can be known through a humanistic interpretation and therefore known through perception suffused with judgment and belief. Science plunges into the phenomena, isolated and apart from the wholeness of reality, interpreting with precision and even accuracy and by devices that make possible more adequate inferences, and sometimes even more reliable predictions, the very same world of things which are antecedently recognized through the implicit perceptions of humanistic insights.

What this Series hopes to demonstrate is that humanism by its nature is intent upon forcing the mind to make, since it is unable not to make, judgments of value. It is to accept once more the validity of the metaphysical hypothesis. What humanism desires and demands is an insight into the meaning of the universe of nature and of man as totality by the use of categories more general or pervasive than those required for the things segmented by a special science. The antihumanist prejudice, prevalent in certain quarters, can be explained only by the dogma that the universe and man in it are everlastingly divided among and by the special sciences, the synopsis of each being separate and exclusive so that a categorial synopsis of the total nature of the thing remains *a priori* precluded.

It is the endeavor of *Perspectives in Humanism* to show that there is no knowledge (knowledge which is synonymous with being) save by a humanistic perception of what we know. For we bring ourselves to every objective act of cognition, we are always intimately involved in every cognitive act. And we can no longer allow ourselves to separate thought from feeling nor to push our subjective experiences into the cognitively irrelevant corner of the emotions (of which poetry, religion, metaphysics, and morality are supposed to be expressions). Knowledge which is at the same time humanistic will then be seen to have a no less legitimate claim than that of any science.

In other words this Series attempts to affirm the truth that man's knowledge can be made relevant to life only by including a knowledge about knowledge. And therefore the humanist can no longer be isolated from the scientist nor can he defend, as he did in the Renaissance, his own studies against the claims of other disciplines. For the humanist even as the scientist has to face the problem of truth, a problem which may be treated in multiple ways, retaining the emphasis, however, on the quest for unity, for that which is constant, in the face of apparently divergent and incompatible doctrines. *Perspectives in Humanism* suggests that one of man's fundamental concerns, be he scientist, philosopher, theologian, artist, or political thinker, is the humanist authority which derives from truth and not the technological authority which derives from power.

Humanism, it is shown here, differs from the specific humanisms of past history in that it forces the mind again and again to recognize wider and subtler relations, lifting seemingly unrelated patterns into a higher harmony. A knowledge of past humanisms is of course indispensable, since some of this knowledge is intrinsically valid and true, and we are summoned to recognize this before we can make significant contributions to our own humanism. This is the heritage each generation is called upon to transmit to the future. It is the humanist heritage which is synonymous with a doctrine of man, explored, enriched, and enlarged for the benefit of mankind and society.

Humanism as presented in this Series affirms the dependence of cultural values on concrete realities. We cannot conceive the former apart from the latter any more than we can conceive a painting apart from its pigment and canvas. And the unity, the constant, in both instances belongs to the realm of values. Therein lie their essence, meaning, and reality. And it is no difficult task to show that those who reject such interpretations in the name of scientific method, of blood, of property, or of economic necessity, and are therefore scornful of humanism as an ineffective phantasm, are themselves actuated to this scorn by dogmas, ideologies, or other value-impregnated thought forms which can come to terms with the former only in the eternal arena of humanistic ideas.

The socialist program of humanism as envisaged by the communists has failed, and henceforth we cannot speak of the problem of Man as having significance only after the collapse of capitalism. For to offer man only what is human is to betray him and to wish him ill, since by the principal part of him which is the mind and the heart man is called to something better than a merely historical or physical life. As Aristotle reminds us, "To propose to man a merely human end is to misunderstand nature."

It is clear that whoever uses the term humanism (and the term itself is ambiguous) brings into play at once an entire metaphysic, and the idea we form of humanism will have wholly different implications according to whether we hold or do not hold that there is in the nature of man a constant, an essence, something which breathes an air outside of time and a personality whose profoundest needs transcend time and space, and even the self.

The authors in this Series try to show that humanism is the essence of all disciplines of the human mind. Humanism indeed tends to render man more truly human. It makes man's original greatness manifest itself by causing him to participate in all that can enrich him in nature and in history by concentrating the universe in man and by dilating man to the universe. This Series endeavors to show how, through humanism, man may make use of all the potentialities he holds within him, his creative powers and the life of reason, and how he may make the powers of the physical world the instruments of his freedom.

The question raised by the authors here is: Can humanism become aware of itself and significant to man only in those moments of despair, at a time of the dissipation of its own energies, of isolation, alienation, loss of identity, dissociation, and descent; only when pain opens man's eyes and he sees and finds his burden unendurable? Does this lead to the proliferation of that atomic anarchy of which Nietzsche has spoken and which Dostoevsky's Grand Inquisitor offers us as a picture of a threatening fate, the nihilism of our time? Is there a humanism conscious of itself and free, leading man to sacrifice and greatness, which is indeed transcendent because here human suffering and consciousness of responsibility open man's eyes? For it is on the humanist answer to this question (and the grounds on which it is decided) that the various positions men take in the face of the travail of history enacted before our eyes and the diverse practical decisions which they feel obliged to make, do in fact depend.

Perspectives in Humanism tries to work toward defining a sound and sane philosophy of modern history so desperately needed. The authors in this Series work to substitute for the inhuman system currently confronting us a new form of civilization which would outline and represent humanism both sacred and secular. *Perspectives in Humanism* tries to show that this humanism is all the more human since it does not worship man but has a real and effective respect for human dignity and for the rights of human personality.

Our age, like every other, is in the grip of its own changing and conflicting thought forms, but the scholar who deals with "facts" cannot achieve objectivity by denuding these "facts" of value, for if he treats them as nonvalues he does not treat them at all. The best he can aspire to is the catholic comprehension and the tolerance that find nothing alien in anything human. Humanism requires that we interpret in our own terms, in the terms of our culture, the total given reality, persistently evaluating it all, means and ends in one, together with the sustaining earth and the indifferent cosmos, and thereby transmuting fact not only into value but also into symbol. This is its necessity, its life, as well as its peril.

The Chinese ideograph, the symbol of humanism, on

the jacket and binding of each volume in this Series is found on early Chinese bronzes in the year 1200 B.C. It reflects the vision and image not of an individual man but of all mankind. It is the symbol chosen for the ability of man to transcend his own isolated self, a quality fundamental to his humanity. The "objectivity" of science cannot help man in his present human predicament, since for science in this sense there can be no commitment. So that in the end we know everything but understand nothing. In fact, we would seek nothing, not being motivated by concern for any question. It is a symbol which is concise, not precise; it is reflective, not descriptive. It is the impersonal self, identical from man to man, and is even perhaps similar to the essence of all life in its manifold expressions in nature. This symbol * thereby shows us why, in our search for meaning, direction, historical unities, and experience in science or in life, we must give logical priority as well as metaphysical preeminence to what we call, for lack of a better term, humanism: that which has something in common with intellectual achievement, with moral action, and with love.

* I am indebted and grateful to Professor Chiang Yee, Professor of Art and Calligraphy at Columbia University. He has generously drawn my attention to this ideograph.

R.N.A.

BUT THAT
I CAN'T BELIEVE!

JOHN
A. T. ROBINSON
BISHOP OF
WOOLWICH

For Elizabeth and Judith

---

who didn't get
HONEST TO GOD

PREFACE

The material that makes up this book was written or spoken at two different levels. The first part, with the exception of the introductory chapter, consists of pieces done for a mass-circulation readership. The second part presupposes a slightly more informed and, with the exception again of its first chapter, a predominantly Christian audience. Each part stands by itself, though the subjects interlock.

I am grateful for permission to reproduce articles from the following papers: *Sunday Mirror* (chapters 2, 3, 5, 7, 8, 9, 11), *Sunday Citizen* (4), *T.V. Times* (6), *The Sun* (10), *Tit-Bits* (12), *New Knowledge* (13), *New Christian* (14, 15, 16, 19, 21, 22, 23). Chapter 11 also appeared in *The Honest to God* debate, ed. D. L. Edwards, S.C.M. Press, London, 1963; chapters 1, 17, 18, 20 and 24 have not been published before.

In each case I have left the material substantially as it was written for the particular occasion. There is therefore no attempt to cover in any coordinated way the whole area of Christian belief. But I suspect that the themes include most of the cardinal points of incredulity!

Finally, I want to thank my wife, Ruth, for some of

the best things in the book, and Marjorie Smith and Stella Haughton, my successive secretaries, who know from the state of my manuscript that, for me at any rate, to write simply is not simple.

— *John Woolwich*

PART I

CHAPTER 1

BUT THAT
I CAN'T BELIEVE!

You can blame it on to Adam,
You can blame it on to Eve,
You can blame it on the apple,
But that I can't believe.
Sydney Carter, FRIDAY MORNING

But that I can't believe! It's a typical reaction to much of Christian doctrine today. And time and again I catch myself saying: "In the sense in which you think you're being asked to believe it, nor can I."

People suppose that being a Christian means swallowing a whole string of statements, of which the following might be samples:

There's a Being called God in heaven who made the world, as a potter makes a pot.

He created Adam and Eve as the first man and the first woman to live on this planet.

They sinned, and we've all been suffering the consequences ever since.

But to save the situation God sent his Son down from heaven to earth.

Jesus hadn't got a human father, but God took the man's part.

As a God-man Jesus could have done anything he wanted to, and sometimes did.

When he died, his body vanished into thin air and was reconstituted as one that could pass through closed doors.

Jesus then went back up to heaven, where we shall go when we die — unless, of course, we are bad, when we shall go to hell.

At the end of the world Christ will be seen returning on the clouds to wind things up.

That's a caricature, but I suspect it's a pretty fair picture of what many people *think* the Church *expects* them to believe.

Certainly when I am asked, "Do you believe in the Virgin Birth or the Resurrection or the Divinity of Christ?" I am aware that the answer "Yes" will be taken by the questioner to mean that I accept that sort of picture more or less literally. The answer "No" will be taken to mean that I'm not a Christian (and therefore ought to resign).

And there are people of very different kinds who see it like this and want to keep it that way.

There are many conservative and middle-of-the-road churchmen who regard one as diluting the Faith or confusing the simple if one can't return a straight "Yes."

Equally, there are powerful vested interests on the other side — humanists who would like Christianity kept as traditional and incredible as possible and regard one as dishonestly slithering out of it if one suggests one simply is not interested in defending the target they know how to knock down.

So one gets caught both ways. But the only thing to do is to pick oneself up again and refuse to be presented with this false either-or.

For the answer I want to give is that I believe profoundly in what these doctrines are concerned to say but that the traditional ways of putting them so often locate the crux at quite the wrong place. One's faith is made to turn on questions to which the answer should well be "Don't know" or even "No." Let me illustrate.

A century ago, as I shall draw out in the next chapter, both traditional Christians and non-Christians were agreed that the truth of Genesis depended on whether Adam and Eve were actual historical characters. One can well understand how those who denied this were thought to be betraying the Faith.

But we can now see that this was really the wrong question. People could give quite different answers to this — and in fact the great majority have now given a negative answer — and still be Christians. For Christianity commits one to a certain interpretation of human nature — which is given classic expression in the Genesis story. It does not commit one to any particular anthropological or biological theory.

In the same way, Christianity stands for a certain commitment to Christ as "God for us." It does not bind us to a particular view of where his genes came from or of what happened to the molecules of his corpse.

As I hope to make clear, I accept as strongly as anyone what the New Testament writers are seeking to affirm by the Virgin Birth or the Resurrection. But I refuse to have this faith made dependent for me or for anyone else on answers to questions which the New Testament doesn't set out to answer, on which there can never be certainty, and on which Christians should be free to differ.

Let me make it absolutely clear that I am *not* saying that a modern Christian *cannot* take these and other miracles literally as physical phenomena. He may well be convinced by the evidence that something quite unusual physically took place.

I myself find the evidence for the empty tomb (which is much stronger documentarily than that for the virgin birth) very compelling. I find it difficult to get away from the fact that the tomb was found empty. But I believe strongly that a Christian can be *free* to say that the bones of Jesus lie around somewhere in Palestine. For the conviction of Christ's living power — which is what belief in *the Resurrection* means — does not *turn* on any theory of what happened to the body.

The same applies to what statements of the Christian faith one takes purely factually as history and what as affirming some spiritual conviction or theological truth.

Consider, for instance, the central clauses of the Apostles' Creed:

a. He was conceived by the Holy Ghost, born of the Virgin Mary.

b. He suffered under Pontius Pilate, was crucified, dead and buried.

c. He descended into hell.

d. On the third day he rose again from the dead.

e. He ascended into heaven.

f. And sitteth on the right hand of God the Father almighty.

g. From thence he shall come to judge the quick and the dead.

Of these, b is a series of straight historical statements. Others, like f, are clearly symbolic expressions of faith. Most are a mixture of both.

On the face of it, all the sentences sound alike and

appear to speak of happenings. But they are certainly not all literal events.

In the past men have not worried very much to ask what *kind* of truth they are asserting.

But today we are acutely conscious of the difference. We cannot lump everything together and simply say "Do you believe this?" without asking a lot of questions. This makes the situation a good deal more complicated. But the same is true of any period of transition — in science or anything else.

Much sifting and counter-questioning is necessary. And the immediate result is bound to appear negative and confusing. For one has to clear the ground so often in order to get down to the real issues.

If the effect of the title of this book, and of some of the things in it, is to suggest that it is primarily about what I *don't* believe, I would assure the reader that he has got it wrong. It's about what I *do* believe — which is also, as I understand it, essentially what the Church of the New Testament and the Creeds has always believed.

For I don't accept that there is such a thing as *a* New Theology (let alone *the* New Theology) — though I am all for new theology, that is, for constantly fresh formulations of the reality of God. And today I believe that these require to be pretty radical.

Trying to do radical rethinking at a popular level involves a double hazard. For it is not simply a case of putting into tabloid language what all the pundits are agreed about. One has to try to be something of a pundit and popularizer at the same time, a backroom boy and a salesman, reworking the sum and not simply dressing up the answers.

It's not a role anyone would choose. I am still by temperament a don rather than a journalist. But it is on the frontier between these two that I am convinced theology has more and more to be done.

It exposes one to the charge of becoming a "pop parson." But I am not in the least interested in accommodating the truth in order to make it palatable. And I find myself quoting William Temple when he was accused of the same thing: "I am not asking, 'What will Jones swallow?' I am Jones asking what there is to eat."

There is a vital difference between really trying to listen to the questions of one's contemporaries, sharing their spiritual hunger, "sitting where they sit" — between that and simply trying to be "with it."

The fine line between the two has been well drawn by Sydney Carter, from whose song I started. On the sleeve of his record, *Songs from ABC Television's "Hallelujah,"* he writes this:

People see the swinging parson, who tries to be both Christian and contemporary, as a tragi-comic figure, rather like a man who thinks he can walk on water.

The twentieth century evangelist, singing *Rock of Ages* to a Beatle tune, is in a desperate position. Can the old wine really go into these new bottles? . . .

Most attempts to modernise hymn books concentrate upon the music, but it is the words, and not the music, that need bringing up to date. Unless the words communicate, all you are left with is a tinkling symbol or a rattling guitar.

Where are the living words that tell the truth in the language of to-day? Not inside the church, perhaps; but outside the church (the Church Visible, at any rate) there are many who are using song to tell the truth . . . The best of them have a standard of integrity, a care for truth, which the Christian must match if he is to be listened to to-day.

It is this test of integrity, of care for truth, which I believe is crucial. Sydney Carter himself is a man who is asking what there is to eat, and asking it in a way that leaves the question with others too. But it is an approach which is the very opposite of jazzing up the old formulae, whether of creed or of code. It involves querying them radically and, maybe, discarding them.

It means, like Jesus, leaving men with as many questions as answers, using the oblique, often ironical, approach of the parable, which forces them to think for themselves. 1463714

Here, as an example to close with, is the complete text of "Friday Morning," quoted with the author's permission. The first commercial record of it was held back for blasphemy! But for me it expresses as nearly as anything the kind of faith through doubt from which I believe most of us have got to be prepared to begin again today.

> *It was on a Friday morning*
> *That they took me from the cell,*
> *And I saw they had a carpenter*
> *To crucify as well.*
> *You can blame it on to Pilate*
> *You can blame it on the Jews,*
> *You can blame it on the Devil,*
> *It's God I accuse.*
> *It's God they ought to crucify*
> *Instead of you and me,*
> *I said to the carpenter*
> *A-hanging on the tree.*
>
> *You can blame it on to Adam,*
> *You can blame it on to Eve.*

You can blame it on the apple,
But that I can't believe.
It was God that made the Devil
And the Woman and the Man,
And there wouldn't be an Apple
If it wasn't in the plan.
It's God they ought to crucify
Instead of you and me,
I said to the carpenter
A-hanging on the tree.

Now Barabbas was a killer
And they let Barabbas go.
But you are being crucified
For nothing, here below.
But God is up in heaven
And he doesn't do a thing:
With a million angels watching,
And they never move a wing.
It's God they ought to crucify
Instead of you and me,
I said to the carpenter
A-hanging on the tree.

To hell with Jehovah,
To the carpenter I said,
I wish that a carpenter
Had made the world instead.
Goodbye and good luck to you,
Our ways will soon divide.
Remember me in heaven,
The man you hung beside.
It's God they ought to crucify
Instead of you and me,
I said to the carpenter
A-hanging on the tree.

CHAPTER 2
ADAM AND EVE

A hundred years ago a raging controversy rocked the Church of England. Three years previously a book had been published called *Essays and Reviews*. Its authors were accused by leading churchmen of "scarcely veiled atheism," of "labouring to destroy and blot out the faith of Jesus Christ from the hearts of the English people."

A public school headmaster (who later became Archbishop of Canterbury) presented a copy of the book to his assistant masters' library. A scandalized letter appeared in a church newspaper — after all, *it might be accessible to the boys!*

When one of the authors, Frederick Temple, was made a bishop five years later, only three of his fellow bishops were willing to take part in his consecration. Another wrote to *The Times* that the appointment was "a blow from which the Church of England may rally for a time, but after which she can never be the same."

A leading humanist said: "You have no business to adopt this reasonable view of the Bible and to remain in the Church." The bishops felt it necessary to issue an episcopal letter to reassure the faithful.

What were these terrible ideas? Here are some that made the most stir:

1. that it might not after all be true that all non-Christians would be everlastingly damned;

2. that Moses was not personally responsible for the first five books of the Old Testament (including the account of his own death!);

3. that the creation story should be understood as myth, not history. In other words, we are not obliged to think of Adam and Eve as *a* particular man and *a* particular woman who were the first human beings to live on earth.

A hundred years ago men who put forward these ideas were vilified by their fellow churchmen. Today we can see that, so far from betraying the Faith, they made it possible for intelligent people to accept the findings of modern science and still to believe in the Bible.

For it is entirely due to the work of men like these that the real meaning behind the Genesis stories has been preserved for ordinary men and women in the 1960s. If we still had to believe that Adam and Eve were the first man and woman on earth, the whole story would be hopelessly discredited.

But communications were slow in the 1860s. There were no popular papers and paperbacks to interpret new ideas, no television and radio to spread them to the farthest corners of the globe overnight.

Even now, the old misunderstandings linger on. A makeup girl in a TV studio asked me the other day: "What do you mean by saying that Jesus was the first man?" She meant Adam, of course; but the century-old problem was still with her.

And for the ordinary person to call something a myth is simply to say that it is *not true.*

But consider, for a moment, myth in modern dress — in the cartoon strip. In place of Adam and Eve, see Andy Capp and his Flo. If I ask you: "Are Andy and Flo real people? Can I find their address and go and look them up?" you'll reply: "Of course not." But can you therefore go on to say: "They're not true"? In a real sense they're only too true.

The reason we can't help shaking our heads affectionately over Andy, despite everything, is *because we recognize him.* For there's more than a little of Andy in each of us. There's none of us that doesn't sometimes want to go through life saying: "I don't want to know."

It's the same with Adam and Eve. They are real, *not because they were actual people, but because they tell us something profoundly true about ourselves.*

After all, Adam is just the Hebrew for Man with a capital M. He's all of us. The Genesis story simply holds up a mirror to life, so that we can see ourselves in it.

How well I remember a scene in my own garden (no need to go to Eden) when my children were young. All the spring bulbs had been trodden under foot.

The characters: the boy next door (also now a bishop's son!), my Stephen, and the cat.

The conversation:

Myself: ??!!

Christopher: Ste'en done it!

Stephen: Mou done it!

Adam and Eve and the serpent! And human nature doesn't change when we grow up and get into trousers.

Can we then after all so readily assert that history is

true and myth is false? Must we not rather say: History records what *did* happen; myth describes what *is* true? Adam and Eve, Andy and Flo, are myths *because* they describe what is true.

Andy and Flo say something true, even if it's trivial, about our human relationships. So a little bit of what they say goes home, even as we laugh at them.

Similarly, Adam and Eve are part of us. We can't get away from them. Go back as far as you will, human nature has always been like that. That's why *in the myth* they are put at the beginning.

But the Genesis stories cut much deeper. For they are not simply about our relationships with each other. They describe, in the language of cartoon strip, the profoundest truths of our being. They speak of our relationship to that reality in which all our lives are rooted, that disturbing presence whom we call God.

And this is not a relationship from which we can opt out. We may prefer not to know; but the love of God will not let us go. "Adam, where art thou?" "Cain, where is thy brother, Abel?"

Still the old questions come through to haunt us — precisely because they were *not* asked just *once* of characters long since dead, but because constantly we hear them addressed to the Adam in each of us.

CHAPTER 3
THE VIRGIN BIRTH

One day recently, a small girl got on her bicycle outside school, swerved, fell on her head and spent several days in the hospital recovering from a concussion.

This, as far as any outside observer could tell, is the whole story of what happened. Certainly, for the young policeman who had to report why an ambulance was called, that is all there was for the record.

But sometimes things that happen to us have a curious knack of highlighting the truth about us. And *to those who know us* these events have a significance beyond the bare facts.

Here, for example, was a little girl who lost her balance and control of her bicycle. But those who know her and love her understand that she has been feeling rather like this about things in general. She hasn't yet found her balance in a new school and doesn't yet feel in control of a strange situation. What is more, her bicycle when it swerved was pointing in the direction of an alternative way home down a main road, which was forbidden, but was the way her friends were going. She was torn both ways, and often is!

Now all this isn't something her parents have suddenly discovered about her. What happened simply spelled out something they already knew to be true.

This, in itself, is a small and insignificant event, except to those concerned. But occasionally something happens which seems to spell out what is true, not only for a few people as individuals, but for all of us human beings.

Such an event was the birth of Jesus Christ.

Indeed, it seemed so important, looking back, that the calendar was calculated from it.

Why did the birth of this Jewish baby seem such a turning point? Because it was an international event at the time? Because there was clearly something miraculous about it? Because it persuaded people there was something different about this man Jesus?

No, not for any of these reasons. Indeed, two of the four Gospels don't even mention it.

Why, then?

Because for the early Christians and for succeeding generations of Christians the story of the birth of Jesus *expresses* what they already know to be the momentous truth about him.

The bare historical fact can be recorded quite simply: a baby, called Jesus, was born in Bethlehem, round about the year we now call 4 B.C.

This, as far as the historian or the outside observer is concerned, is more or less all there is to be said.

But for those who "know their man" there's an inside story, which describes *not necessarily what happened, but what he means for them.*

Consider the story of the Virgin Birth, on which the whole truth of Christianity is often supposed to hang.

Someone I know recently said to me, genuinely puzzled: "But Jesus's mother *must* have been a virgin. If he had had a human father he couldn't have been the Son of God."

But let's be quite clear. This was not the issue for Jesus's followers or for the early Christians.

They were not convinced he was the Son of God because they knew he hadn't a human father or because of anything that happened when he was born.

They were convinced *by what they saw in him.*

He showed them a new kind of living, a new kind of loving, quite out of this world. He seemed rooted in a security that couldn't be explained simply in terms of a human family background.

In him they glimpsed something of the final mystery of life itself. *God* for them shone through him.

And that has been true for Christians ever since. Mystery, wonder, graciousness are realities about Jesus. They are not dependent upon precise historical details, which in any case are shrouded in the past.

But it is natural that these convictions about him should have been woven into the recollection of his birth.

To say that new life was fathered and quickened in Mary by the Spirit of God is a profound way of expressing an inner truth about Jesus. It is to say that his birth and life cannot *simply* be thought of as biological events: his significance lies much deeper than that.

This is what the Virgin Birth is saying, and this is a truth about him which I firmly believe.

With regard to the biological details, I am prepared to keep an open mind. Nothing for me depends upon them.

We do not have to think of Adam and Eve as literal historical figures in order to see that they say something fundamentally true about ourselves.

Equally, we are not bound to think of the Virgin Birth as a physical event, in order to believe that Jesus's whole life is "of God."

A hundred years ago thinking men preserved for us the insights of the Old Testament by disentangling them from certain historical assertions. Had these assertions persisted, the insights would have been discredited.

Perhaps in our generation we are being asked to do the same for the New Testament.

This is *not* to say that all the traditional stories about Jesus's birth are to be swept away as outgrown fairy tales.

On the contrary, they speak to us of something marvelously true about him. Nor do I doubt that they are built around memories of actual incidents.

Imagination is a creative faculty without which we are less than human. Without it we can't entirely grasp truth or share it with each other.

The deepest truths are the most elusive. They are like butterflies — if you try to pin them down you kill them.

That is why the inner meaning of the Christmas history can only be expressed in myth — in the poetry of the angels' song and the wise men's star.

For it is this that conveys to us not simply bare information about incidents long since dead, but their present significance and abiding power.

CHAPTER 4
CHRISTMAS

"But you can't really believe that lot, can you? Stars stopping over cribs, angelic choirs lighting up the skies, God coming to earth as a man — like a visitor from outer space? You couldn't really believe it today. I mean, could you honestly?"

A great many people, I am sure, think like that. And they suppose parsons, and even more bishops, must "believe the lot" — or they wouldn't be where they are. They've a shrewd idea that many of them don't, but that they daren't say so — because their pay depends upon it.

So we get the widespread notion that Christianity and honesty don't mix. I am convinced that this is not true. But I would agree with Dr. Alec Vidler: "We've got a very big leeway to make up because there's been so much suppression of real, deep thought and intellectual alertness and integrity in the Church." I believe that what the world would see above all from the Church is *honesty* — wherever it leads and whatever it costs.

So let me try humbly and honestly to say what I believe — and don't believe — about Christmas.

First of all, what I do believe. What Christmas means to me is that in that baby, and in the man who grew from him, is to be found the clue to the meaning of all life. The Christmas gospel is that what we see in Jesus tells us more about the heart of the universe than anything else. It says that, however it may look on the surface, reality at bottom is like that: love of that quality is the most real, the most powerful, thing in the world.

Now that takes a tremendous amount of believing. In fact, it takes so much believing in the world as we know it that it would be impossible to credit unless in Jesus Christ we have a window through into ultimate reality itself, into God.

And that is what Christmas is claiming — that Jesus of Nazareth is the deepest probe into the meaning of things that we have been given. For in him we reach rock-bottom — that rock of love on which the whole universe is constructed. What we see on the surface of history in Jesus is what it's like at the center. That's what, in traditional language, is meant by the "divinity" of Christ.

And that is the conviction I am passionately concerned that others should share — and act on. And because I am so concerned, I am open to any way of putting it which helps to make it more real. And I am ready to regard as expendable anything that for men and women today makes it unreal — even if it has helped lots of people in the past.

For instance, many today are put off by a way of thinking which was no stumbling block at all to the men of the Bible. They naturally thought of God as "up there" or "out there," and the idea of a heavenly Being "sending" his Son to this world was perfectly acceptable to an age which thought of gods paying visits to the earth. This is where you looked for reality to be revealed. But to most people today that just seems fanciful, and makes the whole Christmas story sound like a fairy tale. I am much more concerned that it shall sound like the reality it is than that we should preserve the time-honored pictures. If it helps to say that in Jesus reality comes through, rather than comes down, then by all means let's say it.

Then there are all the tinselly bits of the Christmas story — the star, the angels, and the celestial choir. These were recognized ways for the men of the Bible of saying "God is in all this." As poetry, I believe, they still have a magic power to take us out of our mean selves. They speak of the mystery of Christmas. But if all they succeed in doing for you is banishing Christ to an unreal world of fairy lights, then cut them out.

Again, the Virgin Birth. If it helps, as it has helped millions, to see in Jesus God at work, well and good. But if it merely succeeds in convincing you that he was not "one of us," then it's much better that you *shouldn't* believe it — for that was never its intention. I'd rather you suspended judgment than let it become a stumbling block.

The main thing I am concerned with is that Christmas should be seen to be about the real world — the world of missiles and housing and unemployment in which we live. Jesus shows us that behind this world — incredible as it may seem — is a love which sets a value on persons that nothing can destroy. And the proof of the Christmas story is in the Easter story. In the end this love is stronger even than death, because that is the way the world is built — Christ's way. We are not just being battered around in an alien universe. The personal purpose behind it comes through to us in Jesus — and claims us for its service. Christians are not people who

succeed in believing six impossible things before break-
fast: they are those who entrust their whole lives to that
claim, in love and compassion and justice for their fellowmen.

CHAPTER 5
MIRACLES

What kind of person do you think Jesus really was?

A miracle-monger, a magic-man, a god in human clothes who could have done anything he liked, if he'd really wanted to?

Or do you reckon he was just a good man — and that all these stories about his divine powers are so much superstitious legend?

Most people imagine these are the only two alternatives. I am convinced they are not.

In the past, the miracles have been taken as evidence that Jesus was divine. Now they merely stop people believing that he was genuinely human. What is a modern person to make of them?

Let's get two things straight with regard to the New Testament itself.

1. The miracles are never used to prove that Jesus was God. Even after one of the most astonishing the reaction was: "A great prophet has arisen among us" and "God has shown his care for his people." In fact, Jesus himself recognizes that his rivals perform cures as much as he does. And he told his disciples

to do the same. Indeed, he said that they would do even greater things than he.

The miracles are seen by Jesus not as things he alone could do because he was divine, but as what any man could do who was really open to the love and power of God.

2. You can't, on any scientific basis, cut out the miracle stories from the Gospels and say that they are later inventions, while the parables and the Sermon on the Mount are original. The evidence for the miracles is just as good, and just as early, as the evidence for the teaching.

Indeed, the two are tied up together. The impression made by Jesus's teaching was precisely that he was, as we should say, as good as his word. "What is this? A new kind of teaching! He speaks with authority. When he gives orders, even the unclean spirits submit." This was love not merely in talk but in action, changing the stunted, tortured lives of men, women, and children.

It's here, I think, that we have the clue for our interpretation. The New Testament words for what we call the miracles are signs, wonders, mighty works. The actions are seen as what becomes possible when the power of love is really let loose.

They are remarkable not because in some arbitrary supernatural way they "break the laws of nature," but because "this is what love can do" when the creative and transforming presence of God is really given free rein.

Consider a typical healing miracle — Jesus curing Peter's mother-in-law. I think my young daughter got to the heart of the matter when, quite spontaneously, she came out with this:

"I know why Peter's mother-in-law took to her bed. I

think she was just fed up with Peter spending all his time going around with Jesus instead of looking after her daughter. *But when Jesus came to her house and she saw the sort of person he was, she wanted to get up and do things for people."*

There's the power of love, overcoming resentment and the physical protest in which it found outlet. And that's why Jesus saw that so often what was needed was a spiritual miracle — the putting right of a person's whole inner outlook on life. And that only love could do, not magic.

Or take the feeding of the multitude, when apparently five thousand men were fed as a result of one boy coming out with his sandwiches. What are we to make of that?

Well, recently five young students went on a trek. They decided that the only way to identify themselves with the starving millions of the world was themselves to go short of food. So they set out from Sheffield over a route of five hundred miles without money and without food. They begged their keep on the way, and talked to people at the same time about the much more desperate need of others. Here is what one of them wrote afterwards:

The feeding of the five thousand is just so true of the world to-day. . . . Trust in that miracle of sharing always started easiest with the young, or with people of no status.

And when we had shared a cup of tea with someone, and literally broken bread into the required number of fair shares, all barriers vanished and we could talk about their problems and ours indefinitely. In fact, that hillside must have been a riot of conversation and laughter two thousand years ago.

"That miracle of sharing" — that's how the story

came alive for a modern young adult on the pulses of her experience. And who shall say she is wrong? For I believe the heart of that story is not the physical miracle of a multiplication of loaves but the spiritual miracle that can be sparked off when even one young person is inspired to share.

And that's what love can do. That's what Jesus could draw out of a person. Time and again what he was able to achieve went beyond anything his contemporaries could account for or explain. Naturally they represented it in the terms of their day as sheer physical miracle.

We may understand more about the workings of spirit over matter — though still how pathetically little! But precisely what happened or how it was done is quite secondary. The important thing, as they recognized, is that in union with the power in which all our lives are grounded there is nothing love cannot do. "With man it is impossible. With God all things are possible."

For the Christian, Jesus is no semidivine wonder-worker. He is a man so completely one with the Father that in him and through him no limit can be set to the power of the Spirit of God. And that, he promised, goes also for all who allow that same Spirit to flood and control their lives.

CHAPTER 6
GOOD FRIDAY

"The New English Bible has brought the words up to date, but the *events* are still as remote as ever." This remark, made to me by someone trying to grasp the significance of Good Friday, puts the problem very aptly.

For the events *are* as remote as ever: indeed, what actually happened in Jerusalem two thousand years ago will recede further and further from us as time goes on. Attempts to recall it by thinking ourselves back into the past and imagining what it must have been like will bring it no nearer.

But this for many is precisely what Good Friday has come to mean. We stand in imagination at the foot of that distant cross, trying to make it real for ourselves by becoming part of the scene, trying to whip up the emotions we think we ought to have experienced if we had been there.

But most of us just aren't up to it. Our imagination isn't agile enough. And because we can't feel ourselves into that event in the past, we either become guilty and oppressed or we dismiss the whole thing as belonging to a world gone beyond recall.

In what sense then, if any, can the death of this man Jesus be other than remote?

Consider, first of all, an event nearer home, any trivial one you like to think of, and ask what is important to you about it.

Suppose, let us say, Grandma comes to stay for Easter. This is an event: it can be prepared for by the family, noted by the neighbors, remembered afterwards. But within the event there is a whole lot more — what you might call the inside story — which is equally real to us: how we felt about her coming, the difference it made having another person in the house, and how everyone reacted to the situation. And when we look back on the visit, it's this, the inside story, that we think of.

What about the inside story of Jesus's death? What did it mean for him, for his friends and contemporaries, and what, if anything, does it mean for us?

With events crowding in upon him during that last week, Jesus might have reacted in various ways. He could have tried to avoid dying for all sorts of good and honorable reasons, by keeping out of the way, by not provoking his enemies, or at least by trying to defend himself. Or he could have resigned himself passively to what was coming to him.

In either case he would have been at the mercy of circumstances: events would have proved too much for him. And in the world's eyes they *were* too much for him: a young idealist needlessly sacrificed to political maneuvering, religious jealousies, and mob hysteria.

But in fact he met the situation quite differently. He accepted what came, not passively, resignedly, but literally with both arms outstretched to take it. Not that he wanted it this way for himself — God! how he didn't want it.

But he refused to be resentful. He accepted and absorbed the evil around him. Love was able to "take it" — and transform it. He went to his death not blaming but forgiving those who were too harassed to know what they were doing.

It certainly wasn't fair. He would have been perfectly justified in feeling bitter against the authorities and toward his friends. And these are the reactions that come naturally to us.

"It isn't fair. We had Gran to stay last time. Let the others take their turn." "Why should I sit back and keep quiet when she does nothing but criticize my hair style and my clothes?" "I can tell when I'm not wanted — you never have appreciated all I have done for you." This might well be the inside story of Grandma's visit.

If these standards had been enough for Jesus, he would still have died. But he would have died because life had proved too much for him and his capacity to love too small. As it was, the love which made him what he was proved too much for death. For this love entered his frightened and despairing followers as a living reality which completely transformed them.

And it has the power to change us too, if we really believe that love *has* the last word over every situation, however tiresome, however unfair, however cruel. For it can accept the tiresomeness of the elderly and the impatience of the young and reassure the hidden fears of both.

If the inside story of Jesus's death can be the inside story of our lives, then we have made his death present. It ceases to be a remote event when it works for us too.

When Christians meet together Sunday by Sunday, and supremely on Easter Day, to break bread and to share the cup over which Jesus agonized the night before he died, this is what they are affirming — that the truth about his death is the truth about their lives.

And this is not because they themselves are determined to make it so, for they will often fail miserably. It is because, underlying what they hope for and despair of in themselves, they are assured that once and for all the case for love has been made and won.

For some weeks now, as I write this, the fans have been listening to a pop singer telling them: "That's what love will do." By the time Good Friday comes, he may have been dropped from the "Top Ten."

But the man on the cross will continue to affirm that same theme — though with infinitely richer power to transform and heal. For, despite what we know in ourselves and see in the world around us, "*That's* what love will do."

CHAPTER 7

THE
RESURRECTION

Christmas is over. Back to reality! We all know the feeling well enough.

The curled up tangerine skin in the hearth, the drip of the red candle wax on the mantelpiece, the daily quota of pine needles on the floor — all that is left to remind us rather sadly of a momentary escape from a humdrum routine.

And now these scattered remnants must be swept up, the glass balls and paper lanterns put away. Once a year is all very well, but you can't live with it forever.

But is this what we *really* feel about Christmas?

A few days off in memory of a man from the past? A few days in which to glimpse what *his* sort of life could mean for us? A time to patch up family quarrels, to open the Berlin Wall, to interrupt bombings? Just one or two days when the spirit of Jesus does play a part in our lives, when he really counts?

Yes — once a year is all very well, but you can't live with him forever!

If this *is* what Christmas means, then, in fact, you don't believe in the Resurrection.

For you the man Jesus remains a memory. You do not

know the thing that "hit" the first disciples, and that transformed a bunch of frightened, disillusioned men into a community capable of changing the world.

For them, too, during those first shattering hours, Jesus had become a memory. He was someone they had known and loved and lost.

They had shared with him a depth of living they had not guessed before. All their hopes for a better way of life were centered in him, and lost with him — buried and sealed in the tomb.

It was all over. They had been quickened by a vision of what life could be, but now they must face life as it was. Back to reality!

And then IT happened. It came to them — rather, as they could only describe it, HE came to them.

The life they had known and shared was not buried with him but alive in them. Jesus was not a dead memory but a living presence.

This is the center of the great historical event which we call the Resurrection.

The very existence of the Christian Church is itself evidence that something irreversible happened to the disciples — *who were expecting nothing of the kind.*

What makes the evidence for the other happenings compelling for us is the extent to which we ourselves share their experience. If we don't share it, we shall probably find them incredible and discard what to us means nothing.

But let's look at these other secondary happenings, for they often loom so large as to obscure the main issue.

Take, first of all, the question of the empty tomb. This, I find, is what most people *mean* by the Resurrection when they ask the question: "Do you believe in the Resurrection?"

But the empty tomb is not the Resurrection any more than the shell of the cocoon is the butterfly. And the real interest of the New Testament is in the butterfly, not the cocoon.

St. Paul's whole gospel, for instance, was centered in Jesus and the Resurrection. But he never once specifically mentions the empty tomb. I have no doubt that he accepted it, but it was not central for him.

What was central for him and for all the early Christians was the compelling conviction that Christ was alive in them. The empty tomb was simply the external sign of what they knew within.

It spelled resurrection only to those who already believed in Jesus. In itself it would have been one more unsolved mystery of crime. In fact, at first it merely filled them with fright and depression.

Precisely what happened to the body we shall never know. The New Testament is silent — and we may be silent too. Believing in the Resurrection doesn't depend on any theory about it.

Some will find it possible and natural to accept a literal vanishing or transformation of the atoms that composed the flesh of Jesus. But even if the corpse was somewhere around, as the cocoon is somewhere around when the butterfly has flown, it was as nothing to his friends any longer.

No one in the New Testament dreamed of instituting a search for the body of Jesus — which would have been the obvious reaction, if only to prove it wasn't stolen or that the women hadn't gone to the wrong tomb.

No, the proof of the matter lay for them within. And it was clinched and expressed for them in what we call the appearances.

Exactly how physical or how psychological these were, I don't think it matters — and the New Testament accounts differ.

Sometimes it was a sudden, startling conviction of Jesus's presence, as tangible as flesh and blood.

At other times it was a more gradual recognition of him behind other eyes and other lips.

But supremely for them, as for succeeding generations of Christians, it was in that act most familiarly associated with him that he made himself known — in the breaking and sharing of bread.

For the truth of the Resurrection is a *present experience*. Belief in it was not confined to those who looked into the tomb or saw the appearances. Nor has it been since. It cannot be proved by historical investigation, but only by a living faith.

To the Christian therefore it is not a question of recapturing a lost memory but of continuing in a reality that death couldn't destroy then — and cannot destroy now.

CHAPTER **8**

THE SECOND COMING

With the Second Coming of Christ we reach what perhaps to most people seems the greatest phantasmagoria in the whole collection of mumbo jumbo that goes under the name of Christian doctrine.

For people really suppose that the Church teaches that one afternoon — this year, next year, sometime — Telstar will pick up a picture of Christ, descending from the skies with thousands of angels in train, returning to earth to judge the world.

But I certainly don't believe that. Nor does any intelligent Christian that I know.

For the Second Coming is not something that can be caught by radar or seen on a screen. It's not a truth like that at all.

It stands for the conviction that — however long it takes — *Christ must come into everything.* There's no part of life from which he can or will be left out.

And to get this truth across, the Bible draws pictures — to make it easier on the imagination.

Thus, there is the familiar picture (painted in glorious technicolor) of the whole world suddenly being flooded with the presence of Christ — as we should say, "out of the blue."

But there are other, more down-to-earth, scenes to bring home the meaning of his coming. At any moment, when you least expect it, he may come into your life — like a burglar at dead of night or the boss walking in when you thought he was on the other side of the world.

This is Jesus speaking, as he constantly did, in parables. No one supposes he'll *literally* knock on the door this evening or enter the office tomorrow morning.

But it makes us stop and think. Suppose our everyday lives were suddenly crossed by his, what should we make of him or he of us?

And it's the same with the other picture of a final blaze of glory. Suppose our lives were transfixed in a flash — just as the H bomb might catch us — and in that moment we had to meet eternity? It too has the power to make us stop and think.

But it too is a picture, a dramatic way of putting it. By this language the Bible is not describing a literal event that is only going to happen once, in the remote or near future — any more than the fall of Adam was a single such event in the past.

To strain your eyes watching the skies for the return of Christ is as misguided as to wait for the archaeologists to dig up evidence for the fall of Adam. For both are ways of trying to make vivid what Christians believe is true not just of one moment but of every moment.

Everywhere, at any moment, *Christ* comes in. That's what the doctrine of the Second Coming is concerned to assert.

The trouble about the phrase "the second coming" is that it suggests that Christ is only coming again once —

and that till then he's well away. But you won't in fact find that phrase in the Bible. It speaks simply of "the coming" of Christ, and the word it uses means "presence."

Always, at every turn, *It's That Man Again!* (I chose that title for the first TV program I ever did, but it was banned by the Independent Television Authority!)

It's that man again! There's simply no getting away from him. You won't meet him, literally, in the high street — or in the clouds. But his life, his standards, his love will find you in the end.

But it's not only in the end, so that we can put off reckoning with him, as we say, "till kingdom come." Even now, he insists on coming in.

Maybe it was in the man you traveled with the other morning in the train, as you turned away and buried yourself in the paper. *Jesus* could have been meeting you in that man's loneliness.

Perhaps it was in the colored couple asking for accommodation. Was there no room for *him* in your home?

But it's not only in our personal choices that Jesus confronts us, but in everything that hits us out of the headlines. The New Testament writers couldn't describe even the most secular, political events without seeing Christ meeting and judging men in them.

We can't help using the word "judging" when we speak of the coming of Christ. For the world is not at ease when he is present — and that is hardly surprising after what it has done to him. No wonder the Bible pictures men as trying to hide their faces from him.

But it shows us another side as well. It pictures men actually inviting him to come. "Come, Lord Jesus!" "Come and stand in the midst of thy disciples and make thyself known in the breaking of the bread!"

Suppose he came back? Christians have no need to suppose. They know he comes back. And above all he meets them at his own board, where he promised his returning presence to his friends. It's as though he said, "You *may* meet me anywhere; but here you will meet me and I shall meet you."

But this particular meeting point is but to *prepare* us to meet him at all points. Shall we know him when he comes? Shall we, next time, be able to recognize his knock? That depends on whether we are used to looking for Christ, on whether we count on him being there.

Watching for the coming of Christ — that's not scanning the skies like Johnny-head-in-air. It's *expecting* Christ to come into *everything*.

You can't believe *that*? Sometimes I wish I couldn't. Life would be a good deal more comfortable!

CHAPTER 9
LIFE AFTER DEATH

I was sitting sometime after midnight in Jimmie's — a dive frequented by students of the University of Chicago. In the course of conversation, a Jewish student said to me through the smoke: "If I could really think, like our fathers, of this life as a mere few seconds' preparation for eternity, it would make a lot of difference. But I can't. Can you?"

I had to agree. I couldn't. There has been a change of consciousness. "Making a good death" no longer strikes people as an intelligent aim in life. It's what they do here that matters. After that the ball can bounce as it will.

Most of us today are not fascinated by death, nor particularly afraid of it. Death has been deflated. Both the horrors and the hopes of anything beyond have lost their power.

I find most churchmen deplore this. But I believe it's simply a difference to be noted about our modern world.

It's largely a question of generation. For many older people, everything turns on what happens after death. If you suggest you don't know — or even don't care — they think you're knocking the bottom out of everything. An ardent Christian student of an earlier generation confessed that if he did not believe in a future life he would rape, murder, steal, and be a drunkard.

The modern young person just doesn't see it like this. In fact he regards such an attitude as positively immoral. What is true or right for him holds whether or not there's anything beyond. He can't get excited by death, and refuses to be obsessed by it.

He doesn't go after spiritualism, playing on the fascination of the beyond. (He may be intrigued by psychical research — but sees no reason to make a religion of it.)

Nor is he sold on "the American way of death" — embalming the loved ones and all that — built on a suppressed striving to deny death.

He plays it cool. Death may be the end. So what? And as for the Christian faith, it must either show itself to be true for this life, or not at all. Its truth can't *turn* on what happens after death. And you can't persuade me into it, he says, by working on that.

I believe this is a healthy reaction. And it's much nearer the Bible. "Though one rose from the dead," said Jesus, "yet will they not believe." Nothing from beyond the grave can of itself settle the issue.

For the men of the Old Testament the word of God was true and the Commandments valid even though they looked forward to nothing further.

For the New Testament eternal life is indeed central. But "this is eternal life" — to know God as revealed in Jesus Christ and in the fellowship of the Spirit. It is a quality of life — here and now — which death cannot touch. Death is put in its place, as powerless to make any difference.

The New Testament doesn't rest its hope on anything *going on* from this life to another. Its confidence doesn't depend on "proofs" of survival such as those produced by the spiritualists. The most they prove is that "vibrations" (if that's the right word) from some people's psyche may linger on and hang around for a time — and there's not much to look forward to in that!

Nor does it say there's a "spark" of immortality in us which never dies. In fact, if one thing is certain, it is that we die. And that's the end of anything that depends on continuities from this body. Belief in the resuscitation of flesh and blood, and consequent religious prejudice against cremation, is sheer superstition.

The Christian symbol of resurrection (rather than of survival or immortality) means that death marks a real break. What lies on the other side of it I literally cannot imagine. And I am not going to be distracted by worrying about it.

All I know is that God lies the other side of it — as he lies this side of it. As the hymn puts it, "He changeth not and thou art dear."

As a Christian, I know my life to be grounded in a love which will not let me go. It comes to me as something completely unconditional. If it could really be put an end to by a bus on the way home it would not have the quality I know it to have.

From such a love neither cancer nor the H bomb can separate. Death cannot have the last word. And "this is the victory — even our faith."

For the rest, with so many of my generation, I am prepared to be agnostic. I just can't imagine an afterlife, and it doesn't help much to try.

To express convictions going beyond sight and touch, the Bible, like all ancient literature, projects pictures (not, of course, intended to be taken literally) of "another world" to which people "go" when they die. Subsequent Christian tradition has elaborated these — and often distorted them.

The pictures are simply ways of trying to make the spiritual truth real and vivid to the imagination. If they help, well and good. But a lot of people today find it difficult to *visualize* anything after death. I am among them.

But our commitment to Christ is not for that reason in doubt. Our concern is with working out that commitment here and now, with what eternal life — real life — means in this situation.

Of course, we can set no bounds to it. As St. Paul says, "If in this life only we have hoped in Christ, we are of all men the most foolish."

But nothing turns on what happens after death. For, whatever happens, we already know a reality we cannot escape and from which nothing can separate.

CHAPTER 10
HELL

"Whatever has happened to hell?" The question was put at a party, where the discussion turned on children's behavior.

The person reporting it to me added: "It appeared that the children we were discussing seemed never to have heard of hell, and some of us recalled that, at our Sunday schools, heaven was the carrot dangled to encourage good, Christian behavior, and hell was held out as the fate of evildoers. Obviously, religious teaching has changed completely."

In that sense, thank God it has. There are still a few who would like to bring back hell, as some want to bring back birching and hanging. They are usually the same types who wish to purge Britain of horror comics, sex, and violence.

Yet the popular presentations of hell were a blatant appeal to horror and violence. There's a medieval mural in a church in my diocese at Chaldon in Surrey, which shows people falling off ladders, with devils waiting to haul them off to boiling caldrons or to saw them up alive.

These were the horror comics of the day — published by the Church. And the worst were positively sadistic.

I say, thank God that's gone. Not even Billy Graham wants to preach hell-fire in the old style. Much of it was sub-Christian — late Jewish or late medieval elaborations of Biblical imagery. And the idea that God creates anyone for eternal damnation — let alone takes delight in it — is itself damnable.

Yet, having said this, I think there is a danger of a real loss of dimension. And it's interesting that though the Church may have stopped talking about hell, the world hasn't.

Wherever you go these days you're hit by flaming letters: "To Hell and Back," "Passport to Hell," "See You in Hell, Darling."

It's worth noting incidentally that all these are adult films, and not family films. Hell is an adult subject. Don't let us subject children to it. They will discover in their own time that life can be hell — though we can prepare them for it.

For that is really what hell is about — the dark side, the shadow side, of life. And no view of the world, certainly no gospel, that doesn't reckon with that can be other than shallow and sentimental.

You hear people saying: "It's been hell" or "I really went through hell." What kinds of experiences prompt such language? I think there are three.

1. Experiences of suffering, frightfulness, and torture — physical or mental. Some things are so ghastly that they can only be described as "hell on earth" or "a living hell."

2. Experience of madness — when reality, or the loss of reality, becomes unendurable. Many representations of hell have in fact been psychotic — descriptions of a nightmare world.

3. Experiences of alienation — of being up against it in a relationship from which one cannot get away. A marriage can be "sheer hell." "Hell," says Sartre in one of his plays, "is other people."

All these are experiences which are real enough. They are not invented by theologians. What Christian theology does is to interpret every aspect of human life in the light of the final reality of God's love. And in so doing it gives a new dimension both to its height and to its depths. The full meaning of life is heaven that the world cannot imagine and hell that it hardly knows.

The trouble has been that both heaven and hell have been pictured as places rather than states, and located simply the other side of death. Of course, for the Christian, they are realities that are not *ended* by death. But all he can usefully say about them is from his present experience.

In a real sense the definition of heaven and hell is the same: being with God — forever. For some that's heaven, for some it's hell: for most of us it's a bit of both.

The Christian believes that life has a grain running through it. The world is made a certain way — for love. To try to live one's life across it is ultimately hell: there is no peace that way.

But the grain is not like something in wood. It's more like something in a person. And to be across a person in whom eternally one lives and moves and has one's being is a most ghastly prospect. It is Sartre's "hell is other people," only more so.

People have experienced hell in different ways. Some have felt it as sheer dereliction, as dropping out of God's love into a dark and meaningless abyss. Hence those ladders in the mural.

Others have found the reality they cannot tolerate only too close. It burns them up. It lacerates them.

I do not believe in a God who is content for any finally to live with him and find it hell. But I cannot take the love of God — or for that matter human love — seriously without taking the agony of it equally seriously.

In that sense I believe in hell. It's no kindness to encourage anyone to think that life can be lived at any depth without the shadows. Being in love — and that's what the Christian thinks is our ultimate element — is a searing process.

But God forbid that we should use hell as a stick to keep anyone moral.

CHAPTER 11
NEW THEOLOGY

Some years ago Mr. Gaitskell proposed revising the famous Clause Four (on nationalization) of the Labour Party's constitution.

Mr. Wilson, who opposed him, dubbed it all "theology" — theoretical statements about things that make no practical difference.

Such is the name that theology has gained. But suddenly that image seems to have changed.

Up till now the press took notice of clergymen only if they spoke on morals or politics. What they said on God and the Gospel was ignored. Archbishop William Temple constantly complained of this. But now "God" is news.

Honest to God seems to have touched people at a point where truth really matters to them. And of that I am glad — even if it has meant some pain.

For God is to be found at the point where things really do matter to us.

What drove me to write the book was that this is simply not true for most people.

What matters to them most in life seems to have nothing to do with God; and God has no connection with what really concerns them day by day.

At best he seems to come in only at the edges of life. He is out there somewhere as a sort of outfielder — at death, or to turn to in tragedy (either to pray to or to blame).

The traditional imagery of God simply succeeds, I believe, in making him remote for millions of men today.

What I want to do is not to deny God in any sense, but to put him back into the middle of life — where Jesus showed us he belongs.

For to the Christian God is not remote. He is involved; he is implicated. If Jesus Christ means anything, he means that God belongs to this world.

So let's start not from a heavenly Being whose very existence many would doubt. Let's start from what actually is most real to people in everyday life — and find God there.

What is most real to you? What matters most for you? Is it money, and what money can buy?

I doubt it, deep down. For you know that you "can't take it with you." And seldom does it bring real happiness.

Is it love? That's a good deal nearer, because it has to do with persons, not things.

But what is love? Sex? Sex is a marvelous part of it. But sex by itself can leave people deeply unsatisfied. Remember Marilyn Monroe?

We all need, more than anything else, to love and be loved. That's what the psychologists tell us. But by that they mean we need to be *accepted* as persons, as whole persons, for our own sake.

And this is what true love does. It accepts people, without any strings, simply for what they are. It gives them worth. It "makes their lives."

That is precisely what we see Jesus doing in the Gospels, making and remaking men's lives, bringing meaning back to them.

In him we see love at work, in a way that the world has never seen before or since.

And that's why the New Testament sees God at work in him — for God is love. In the cross that love comes out to the uttermost. "There's love for you!" says Calvary.

And in the Resurrection we see that not even death was able to destroy its power to transform and heal. Love still came out on top.

The Christian is the man who believes in *that* love as the last word for his life.

It is quite simply for him the ultimate reality: it is God.

The universe, like a human being, is not built merely to a mathematical formula. It's only love that gives you the deepest clue to it.

"It's love that makes the world go round." That's what all Christians have always said. But so often they have *pictured* it in a way that makes it difficult for modern man to see it.

They have spoken as though what makes the world go round were an old man in the sky, a supernatural person.

Of course, they don't take that literally. It helps only to make God easier to *imagine*. But it can also hinder. Perhaps a comparison will show what I mean.

The ancient Greeks thought of the earth being upheld on the shoulders of a superman called Atlas. That was their way of saying that it doesn't support itself in space.

We also know that it doesn't. For us it is held in orbit by the sun's gravitational pull.

The ancient myth was saying something true. But such language today would not convey the truth to a modern man. It would be much more likely to conceal it.

So with Christian truth. The reality is that in Jesus we see the clue to all life. To say that he was the son of a supernatural Being sent to earth from heaven may help to bring this home.

But for others it may take it out of their world altogether — so that the events of Christmas and Holy Week seem to belong to a religious fairy story.

If the traditional way of putting it makes Christ real for you — the most real thing in the world — well and good. I don't want to destroy anyone's image of God.

I wrote my book for those who have increasingly come to feel that it makes him unreal and remote.

I tried simply to be honest about what God means to me — in the second half of the twentieth century.

The hundreds of letters I have received, particularly from the younger generation, inside the Church and out of it, have convinced me that I may have rung a bell for others too.

For that I can only be humbly thankful.

For I want God to be as real for our modern secular, scientific world as he ever was for the "ages of faith."

CHAPTER 12
NEW MORALITY

"The new morality!" A little time ago, hardly anyone had heard the phrase.

Now it is bandied about from pulpit, press, and platform. And for most people it means simply one thing: easy sex — "the old immorality condoned," as Lord Shawcross tartly put it.

And I am supposed to have invented it!

First, let's get the record straight.

"The New Morality" was a chapter title in *Honest to God*. But I put it in quotes. For it was not my phrase, but the Pope's (not of this one but of the one before last).

Not that he liked it. He didn't. But as he used it — and I used it — it had nothing particularly to do with sex.

For me it meant that you can't lay down in advance absolutes of right and wrong for all occasions, and then fit persons to them. For "the Sabbath is made for man, not man for the Sabbath." Persons are more important than principles.

I didn't think I was saying anything especially new. And in fact for the first three months that chapter in my book aroused practically no comment or controversy —

despite the fact that usually it's morals, not theology, that makes news.

Then it all got mixed up in the summer scandals of 1963. Mr. Profumo was asserted, in a letter to the Church press, to have taken my advice — though not interestingly enough on sex, but on lying to Parliament! Which only goes to show how everything in English discussion gets channeled sooner or later into one groove.

Since then the same label has been stuck indiscriminately on everyone — Christian and non-Christian alike — who has uttered on the subject, as though we were all saying the same thing.

But there are vast differences between us. Let me simply state my own concern.

I want people to be *free* — to decide responsibly for themselves what *love* at its deepest really requires of them. But there could hardly be anything further from that than free love — which is usually neither love nor free.

Consider, for instance, this conversation from the film *Room at the Top:*

"I do love you," she protests; "I would do anything for you." "Sure," he retorts, "you would do anything — except the one thing any girl would do for the man she loves." So she succumbs — the victim of emotional blackmail.

That's not love. It's much more fear than love — fear of losing him if she doesn't.

Under that sort of fear people are not free. And thousands of young people today are simply being played upon in this matter of sex.

Their emotions are exploited by the advertisers. Glamour is commercialized. They can't afford not to go along with the rest. "Dread of being a social outcast is the main reason why teenagers have sexual intercourse before marriage," writes a girl student in *Sixth Form Opinion*.

I want a morality which frees people from that. But I know we shan't get it by simply saying "Thou shalt not!" a bit louder.

Young people today ask "Why?" — and quite rightly. They want a basis for morality that makes sense in terms of personal relationships. They want *honesty* in sex, as in everything else.

And that's what chastity is. It isn't just abstinence. It's honesty in sex: having physical relationships that *truthfully express* what's there underneath.

Sex — and this applies inside marriage just as much as out of it — which doesn't really express love is an immoral sham.

But what is love? It's giving yourself to the other person, completely and without condition, for his or her own sake. It's wanting to share your whole life, without keeping anything back.

Sex is the most intimate and wonderful expression of this deep sharing of life with life. To use it for kicks — or out of fear of being thought a square — when there's nothing there behind it is a fearful desecration.

But suppose there *is* something there? Suppose you are deeply in love, but can't get married?

I would say: "Be absolutely honest with yourself." Even if you're engaged, you can't really share everything. Bed without board *is* a cheat — especially for the girl. If you *really* love her, you'll think twice — and twice again. For it's bound to be less than the best.

But it's your decision. I'm not going to take it for you or take it from you. I can know what love demands of me. But, no more than Jesus, am I going to throw the first stone into other people's lives — though I can do my utmost to save them from messing them up.

I believe that young people today are genuinely looking for a morality that cuts deeper, is more searching and less superficial than the ready-made rules of their parents — honored in any case more in the breach than in the observance.

As Sir Edward Boyle, a former Minister of Education, has said, "Never has there been more serious discussion of the human love relationship than is going on today. . . . I believe young people can be brought to realize that a close personal relationship can be either the most life-enhancing and joyous or, alternatively, the most destructive thing on earth."

And in all this they desperately need *help,* not condemnation. I prefer to keep my condemnation for:

1. Those who exploit sex for gain — especially under the nauseating hypocrisy of "exposing vice."
2. Those who tell the young that they can't be "with it" unless they "have sex."
3. Those who treat sex simply as a game (which is different from saying that there is a playful element in it to be enjoyed).
4. Those who snigger at it as dirty or moralize about it as sin.
5. Those who report what responsible people say as though they were advocating immorality or condoning laxity.
6. Those who weigh in with a heavy hand on the basis of such press reports.

Finally, I want to *commend* those who are trying to hammer out real standards for their lives amid so many more pressures than we were exposed to. And I want to commend those — only too few — who are prepared to give of their time to get alongside them in schools and clubs, at home and in church, in clinics and counseling.

For this is where any new morality must be thrashed out which is really going to be worth anything.

PART II

CHAPTER 13
DO WE NEED A GOD?

An American magazine is reputed to have sent a telegram to Einstein: "DO YOU BELIEVE IN GOD STOP PREPAID FIFTY WORDS." Asked, "Do we need a God?" I am inclined to reply on a postcard: "If the question is put like that, no."

First, however, let me say that it is a good question. For it reflects well enough what people actually ask. But I should want to go on to insist that it's a bad question, if one is looking for a simple answer that gets to the truth of the matter. For the question of God as ordinarily put is hardly any longer about the real issue. No wonder people are confused.

It has been said that "the creed of the English is that there is no God and that it is wise to pray to him from time to time." Ostensibly, however, the creed of the English is emphatically that there *is* a God (the latest opinion poll gave 84 percent for, with only 2 percent definitely against) and that it is wise to pray to him from time to time (43 percent, incredibly, said "regularly"); but their other answers show that in terms of that God they are practical atheists.

The polls merely reflect the fact that somehow the

traditional question has ceased to be the relevant one. Reverse the percentages and one would get an equally plausible picture. People say yes because there's something they don't wish to be put in the position of denying, when the truer answer might be no. Conversely I, who find the reality of God inescapable, would doubtless be recorded among the 16 percent doubtfuls or unbelievers if asked for a straight yes or no to the question "Do we need a God?"

The reason I would jib is summed up in the two little words "need" and "a." To explain will help to clear the ground for what I believe to be the real question.

First, do we *need* a God? The whole history of the past two hundred years has been a questioning of the need to bring God into one department of life after another. When in the eighteenth century Newton wrote about physics and Kant about ethics, both believed that God was necessary in order to round off their systems — for Newton, to intervene and regulate the planets' motions; for Kant, to ensure that virtue was in the end matched with happiness. God was a necessary hypothesis, even in a rationalistic age.

The revolution of the nineteenth century is represented by the famous remark of the mathematician Laplace, when asked by Napoleon where God fitted into his system: "Sir, I have no need of that hypothesis." In other words, scientific explanation can be complete without having to introduce God. And today we all accept this. It is simply bad science to resort to God to fill the gaps. And for religious people to resist this process, to suppose that room can be found for God only by keeping open a space in the circle of explanation or control, is merely to ally faith with ignorance.

But it is not simply in the field of intellectual explanation that God has ceased to be needed. Marx and Freud in their different spheres have revealed the extent to which the figure of God has been used as a compensation or projection. Religion has been a prop or a sop. Men have run to God, expecting him to intervene or to correct the balance (here or hereafter) in a way that has merely revealed their emotional immaturity.

One of the effects of secularization has been to compel man to take responsibility for his destiny in matters which before could be left "in the lap of the gods." For good or for ill, he has "come of age." One of the most influential of Christian voices today, that of Dietrich Bonhoeffer, hanged by the Nazis in 1945, warned against resisting this in the name of God, and against exploiting needs in the last recesses of the soul which only "God" could answer. For this once again is to ally faith with man's weakness and ignorance rather than with his maturity.

For these reasons I would refuse to test the truth or falsity of the reality of God by whether or not it can be shown that we *need* him.

I would have equal reservations about the expression *a* God. For *a* God is almost by definition no God — a puppet, an idol created by the finite imagination of man.

From time immemorial men have projected their deepest spiritual convictions and values on the heavens and have visualized beings who embodied them in some supernatural realm above or beyond this one. This is a process we recognize readily enough, say, of the gods of ancient Greece and Rome. No one seriously believes these gods "existed," on the top of Olympus or anywhere else. The realities of Greek and Roman religion, however, remain — insights into the deepest things of life from which we can still learn, as we can from the art or philosophy of the same cultures. The projection, the description, of these insights as beings inhabiting another, separate world of their own is now recognized as a human creation, a personification in terms of superhuman characters of the profoundest realities of religious experience. We can acknowledge this without questioning the realities they sought to represent.

In the same way, the conception of God as *a* Being, a Person — like ourselves but supremely above or beyond ourselves — will, I believe, equally come to be seen as a human projection. (Most people already recognize this in the case of the Devil.) It is a way of making real and vivid to the imagination, by personification, the conviction that reality at its deepest is to be interpreted not simply at the level of its impersonal, mathematical regularities, but in personal categories such as love and trust, freedom, responsibility, and purpose. *The real question of God is not whether a Being exists whom we visualize as embodying this in his Person. It is whether this conviction about the ultimate meaning of things is true.*

It is quite possible that we may *not* need a God, any more than a Devil. For most people till now such a supernatural person has in fact been an indispensable focus for the imagination, both in prayer and in communicating the reality to others. But then most people till now, at any rate in the West, have lived in a universe divided mentally into two realms, a natural and a supernatural.

But though it may have helped — and many would regard it as unexpendable — I am convinced that this projection of God as a Being in another realm has equally succeeded in making him marginal to vast numbers of people today. They cannot recognize the reality of God in experience because the image which should be making it vivid locates him in an area in which they no longer "live." He is banished to the edges of life — to the uncanny (the significance now of the supernatural), to what men still cannot understand or control (so-styled acts of God), or to what is revealingly called the afterlife. People turn to him at the end of their tether; but in the ordinary course of affairs he comes in, if at all, only after the vital connections have been made. In fact, once again, almost by definition he has ceased to be God. Consequently it has become insignificant whether 84 percent of the English say they believe in him or 16 percent.

Having thus tried to clear the ground, I come to what I believe is the real question — not "Do we need a God?" but "Can we finally get away from the reality for which the word God has stood?"

God stands, as the medieval Scholastic philosophers insisted, for the *ens realissimum,* the most real thing in the world. The word relates to what is most deeply true and real, to what is of ultimate concern and significance.

Now there are obviously various levels at which we can view reality. Human beings, for instance, can be interpreted perfectly validly from the point of view of the physicist or the chemist, in terms of the same patterns of vibration and molecular composition as any other matter. But this tells us little distinctively about them as men and women.

The sociologist or psychologist can add information that takes us a good deal further into what makes human beings what they are. But the relation in which the analyst or social scientist stands toward his subject is still an impersonal one.

We get down, as we say, to "the real person" only when this I-It approach yields to an I-Thou relationship in which he ceases to be an object of inquiry and is met as a subject in and for his own sake, in friendship, love, and trust. It is only at this level that we can truly know a person (as distinct from knowing about him) and the real depths and heights of human existence are disclosed.

In the same way, the universe discloses its true nature at different levels. At one level the world can be understood and controlled in terms of its mathematical regularities. Indeed, at this level it is possible in theory to give a complete explanation. Certainly, as I insisted at the beginning, the believer has no interest in finding a place for God in the gaps of such explanation — any more than the truth of the I-Thou relationship with persons depends on holes in the scientist's analysis.

But no pattern of mathematical regularities, however complete, can provide values or quality or meaning. Unless there are realities in the universe deeper than these, to which the mind and spirit of man responds, then all features of life which distinguish human beings from the animals — civilization, art, ethics, science itself — rest on no more than subjective attitudes of the kind: "I like mustard; I don't." But the artist, the reformer, or the scientist speaks characteristically of a claim upon him to which he must be faithful. And this presents itself with the same givenness as the quantitative aspects of the universe — as a reality once sensed from which he cannot get away without selling out.

The level of reality for which men have required the word God is one that presupposes and underlies all these others. It is evidenced in the response to the sacred, the holy, the absolutely unconditional: "Here stand I: I can do no other." It comes with the same sense of inescapable, compelling objectivity — of something profoundly disturbing yet profoundly gracious, ultimate yet intimate.

It comes in many forms — in the "Thus saith the Lord" heard by Isaiah or Jeremiah; in Wordsworth's "sense sublime of something far more deeply interfused"; in the haunting Alleluias of Stravinsky's *Symphony of Psalms;* in the testimony of mystics and prophets, saints and ordinary men and women the world over.

This is the reality which the believer finds it impossible to deny. He may not "need" it — though he discovers his life fulfilled in it. He may not represent it as "a" Person — though the nearest analogy in his experience is the kind of claim that meets him in personal relationships. But, however dimly perceived or obeyed, it is for him, as supremely it was for Jesus, the reality in whose grace and power the whole of his life is lived.

CHAPTER 14
GOD DWELLING INCOGNITO

The God dwelling *incognito* at the heart of all things: such is the theme of what seems to me one of the most remarkable novels of our time, and one curiously ignored so far for its contribution to the current theological ferment. It is by the Roumanian ex-communist, Petru Dumitriu, and is simply called *Incognito*.[1] In the tradition of *The Brothers Karamazov* and *Doctor Zhivago,* it is a profoundly moving account of the quest for sanctity and humanity in and through and beyond the corruptions and inhumanities of life in our generation.

Its theology is unashamedly pantheistic — or, more accurately, panentheistic. God is in everything and everything is in God — literally everything, material and spiritual, evil as well as good. The voice of my education tells me that by the canons of othodox Christian theology it is doubtless heretical. One is inclined to reply, so much the worse for orthodox Christian theology. But at any rate orthodox Christianity must *listen*. For there is an intensity of spiritual power and love here which could

[1] English translation by Norman Denny (Collins, London; The Macmillan Co., New York — 1964).

make this book a classic of twentieth-century mysticism. Deeply rooted in Eastern European spirituality, it nevertheless represents a worldly holiness and a holy worldliness which speaks straight to the condition of Western, Bonhoefferian man.

It is worth asking, first, *why* pantheism is suspect from a Christian point of view. In its familiar forms, whether of Indian religion or of Western intellectualism, it tends toward an aesthetic, impassive, impersonalistic view of life in which the individual loses his significance. It makes for an unhistorical quietism, without political cutting edge or involvement with the neighbor. Above all, it plays down evil and suffering as partial or illusory: it has little sense of judgment or sin. "O help us to see," says the wonderfully complacent pantheistic hymn gaily sung by those who have wallowed in Cranmer's confession, " 'Tis only the splendour of light hideth thee."

Nothing could be further removed from the atmosphere of Dumitriu's book. Here we are in an intensely personalistic world, in which everything depends upon the utterly individual response of love. Indeed it is this that gives the world its meaning and makes it possible to speak in terms of God at all.

This was it, the sense and meaning of the universe: it was love. This was where all the turns of my life had been leading me. And now everything was truly simple, revealed with a limpid clarity to my eyes as though in a flash of light *illuminating the world from end to end,* but after which the darkness could never return. Why had I needed to search so long? Why had I expected a teaching that would come from outside myself? Why had I expected the world to justify itself to me, and prove its meaning and purity? It was for me to justify the world

---

by loving and forgiving it, to discover its meaning through love, to purify it through forgiveness.[2]

And yet equally clearly it was not "I" imposing my meaning, my love on an alien universe. This love was essentially *response,* welling up "from some unknown source that was not me but *thou.*"

What name was I to use? "God," I murmured, "God." How else should I address Him? O Universe? O Heap? O Whole? As "Father" or "Mother"? I might as well call him "Uncle." As "Lord"? I might as well say "Dear Sir," or "Dear Comrade." How could I say "Lord" to the air I breathed and my own lungs which breathed the air? "My child?" But he contained me, preceded me, created me. "Thou" is his name, to which "God" may be added. For "I" and "me" are no more than a pause between the immensity of the universe which is *Him* and the very depth of our self, which is also *Him.*[3]

This illumination of unspeakable meaningfulness at the heart of everything comes in the novel only after nearly three-quarters of it has elapsed, and at the moment of most utter dehumanizing degradation and torture.

They went on beating me, but I learnt to pray while the screams issued mechanically from my ill-used body — wordless prayers to a universe that could be a person, a being, a multitude or something utterly strange, who could say? We say "Thou" to it, as though to a man or animal, but this is because of our own imperfection: we may no less say "Thou" to the forest or the sea. We say "Thou" to the universe and hear its voiceless answer in our hearts as though it were a person and had heard us.

[2] P. 354.
[3] P. 356.

But it is He who prays within us and answers the prayer which is His gift.[4]

It is the ability to take up *evil* into God and transform it that is the most striking — and shocking — feature of this theology.

"But you're giving the world the name of God, which is monstrous!" cried Erasmus.

I asked if it was monstrous of me to call him Erasmus. I used the name of God because it was a way of directing towards the world all the worship, veneration and prayer which our forebears had devoted to gods growing increasingly less circumscribed; until they became the God of the monotheistic religions, defined by the universe, or by evil, or by His own goodness and perfection, or by reason. Erasmus burst out:

"You must be mad! Do you mean that this God of yours is not perfect?"

"Yes. He is perfect, but He is also terrible and evil. He is both perfect and imperfect. He is all things, and He confines himself to none." [5]

God is in everything — literally. All things, all events, all persons are the faces, the incognitos of God. This naturally brings protest.

"In fact, you're nothing but an atheist," he said. "You've no real religious feeling at all. To include evil and imperfection in the concept of God is outrageous and immoral!" I answered that the idea of a single God had at one time been attacked in similar terms, and that I could not disregard what I had seen with my own eyes in the course of my life.[6]

It is this refusal to exclude any experience from the raw material of theology that is courageous in its honesty if nothing else.

[4] P. 358.
[5] Pp. 403–404.
[6] P. 405.

God is everything. He is also composed of volcanoes, cancerous growths and tapeworms. But if you think that justifies you in jumping into the crater of an active volcano, or wallowing in despair and crime and death, or inoculating yourself with a virus — well, go ahead. You're like a fish that asks, "Do you mean to say God isn't only water, He's dry land as well?" To which the answer is, "Yes, my dear fish, He's dry land as well, but if you go climbing on to dry land you'll be sorry." [7]

What is required is not to accept everything as it stands but to "vanquish lethargy" by the seemingly impossible response of love.

What is difficult is to love the world as it is now, while it is doing what it is doing to me, and causing those nearest to me to suffer, and so many others. What is difficult is to bless the material world which contains the Central Committee and the *Securisti;* to love and pardon them. Even to bless them, for they are one of the faces of God, terrifying and sad.[8]

Yet

If I love the world as it is, I am already changing it: a first fragment of the world has been changed, and that is my own heart. Through this first fragment the light of God, His goodness and His love penetrate into the midst of His anger and sorrow and darkness, dispelling them as the smile on a human face dispels the lowered brows and the frowning gaze.[9]

All around me the divine machinery of evil pulses like the plunging of pistons — cruelty, vengefulness, greed, envy, stupidity, selfishness, arrogance. And mingled with them are gentleness, innocence, friendship, trust, solidarity, fidelity, mother-love and the love of lovers, charitable

[7] P. 407.
[8] P. 458.
[9] P. 459.

work, serenity of spirit, prayer and holiness. I have been merged in the town and the things that make the town, people, buildings and machines, all the devices of civilisation, which are as much a part of God as the rose or the earthquake, the shoal of fish or the work of art. Nothing is outside God. I have sought love in such a fashion that love flowing out of me will spread as far as may be. I have tried to keep within the radiance of God, as far away as possible from His face of terror. We were not created to live in evil, any more than we can live in the incandescence that is at the heart of every star. Every contact with evil is indissolubly linked with its own chastisement, and God suffers. It is for us to ease His sufferings, to increase His joy and enhance His ecstasy. I made friends in the crowd, at meetings, in the sports stadium and coming out of the cinema, as a rule only for a moment, linked with them by a friendly exchange of words, a smile, a look, even a moment of silence. And in closer contacts my discovery spread slowly but constantly from one person to another, in that dense and secret undergrowth which is wholly composed of personal events.[10]

It is this fellowship of the "secret discipline" of love that constitutes the invisible leaven of the Kingdom. For that no labels are necessary — not even the Christian one — and any structure kills it. This provokes the natural exasperation of the organization man:

"But what are we supposed to do?" he demanded in some irritation. "Tell me in explicit terms. What's your programme?"

I said that those who love rightly always know what to do; that sacred love shapes our inward bearing like a flame in a wax world, which melts it and gives it a new form.

"That's all so vague and foggy! Why don't you say to me, 'Do this and don't do that'?"

"Do you expect orders to come to you from outside?

[10] Pp. 431–432.

Are you one of those who expect God and the answer to their questions to be outside themselves? . . . I can't give you any commandments of that sort. At the most, only this — cause no one to suffer. Never give way to apathy or indifference. Do what love impels you to do. Do not lie to yourself about what is truly love in your heart and what is not."

"It's still so vague," he muttered. "And what are you going to do? How do you propose to organise this action?"

I was growing more and more perturbed. I wondered what sin I had committed. An unexpected melancholy was taking possession of me.

"I don't propose to at all. Any kind of organisation would involve us in the machinery of determinism, a dialectic outside the individuality of each of us. Do you want yet another Party? Or another Church?" [11]

This is essentially a theology of the latent, rather than the manifest, Church. And we should listen to it as that, rather than criticize it for what it is not. There is nothing specifically or exclusively Christian about it. But there is one explicit reference to Christ on which it is fitting to end:

It was in that cell, my legs sticky with filth, that I at last came to understand the divinity of Jesus Christ, the most divine of all men, the one who had most deeply and intensely loved, and who had conceived the parable of the lost sheep; the first of a future mankind wherein a mutation of human hearts will in the end cause the Kingdom of God — the Kingdom, Tao, Agarttha — to descend among men.[12]

[11] P. 428.
[12] P. 383.

CHAPTER 15

BEARING THE REALITY OF CHRISTMAS

It is not often that one remembers a Christmas card twelve months later. But last year I was sent one that has stuck in my consciousness ever since.

It was simple in the extreme — a black and white photograph, taken for the Save the Children Fund, of a Jewish family not far from Bethlehem. The three of them are sitting against a wall, surrounded by all their worldly wealth in a few packing cases. On top of one the father, who is a cobbler, is plying his trade. On another, with her little boy close against her, sits the mother in a shawl. Between her hands she is holding a creased bank note and gazing thoughtfully through it, as though pondering how far it could be made to go. That is all, and underneath a quotation from the poet Coventry Patmore: "I have many things to say to you, but you cannot bear them now. Not because they are so unlike your mortal experiences, but because they are so like."

Why, I have asked myself, did that card speak to me as no other did? I got many gayer, many more exciting, many of finer art. Yet somehow we have reached the point — or I have reached the point — when all the art, all the design, all the poetry, picture, story and myth, however beautiful, contrive as often as not to dim the reality of Christmas rather than add to it.

And above all our generation wants *reality*. It has a hunger and a craving for it. It may not be able to bear it when it gets it. As T. S. Eliot said, "Human kind cannot bear very much reality." I know I can't. I secretly funk going to India. I don't know whether I could stand watching men and women and children literally starving to death in the streets. But I know that no faith, no way of life that does not take this reality seriously is any help. I know there are many things I cannot bear — not because they are so unlike our mortal experiences but because they are so like. And Christmas, stripped down, is one of them. And yet I know that this is the Gospel, if we can bear it.

What I also know, speaking for myself, is that the poetry, the imagery, the magic of Christmas has largely now the opposite effect. For so many of our generation, instead of increasing the dose of reality to the point at which it hurts and heals, it contrives to make it all so *unlike* our mortal experiences. It seems to take it out of our world altogether.

That was not the original intention of such language at all. The men who wrote the New Testament were men who had known Jesus as one of themselves. They had no illusions about their experiences being his and vice versa. That photograph could for them have been of him — literally. The language in which they told the Christmas story — of skies opening and stars guiding, of angels coming and going, of divine intervention and heavenly conception — was not intended to sever the link with the world of everyday occurrence. It was simply their way of indicating the *significance* to them of this astonishing man. It was to say that if you look through this otherwise ordinary event — as the mother is looking through her very ordinary bank note — and turn it over and over and ponder it, you will see in it and beyond it something tremendous. It speaks of what, deepest down, reality is like, of what finally is true, of what ultimately matters and gives meaning to life — in other words, of God. In these events they felt they had struck rock, they had met what was for them the most real thing in the world, the *ens realissimum*. As they confessed afterwards, *"God* was in Christ."

And in their supernaturalistic age they described this, communicated this, in the only way they knew — by giving the whole story a glow of glory, a brush of wings, a touch of sheer miracle. The descriptions were there to give the *interpretation* of the events, the unfathomable depth of significance they had seen in the happenings they had been part of. Just what in the story they told of this child's birth is event and what interpretation is to me of minor importance. Both event and interpretation are present and both are necessary — and different people will separate the mixture differently. What I *am* concerned about is that we shall see the poetry, the myth, for what it is intended to be — a way of describing the meaning, the ultimate divine significance of the history — and not a literal account of *how* things happened. The birth stories begin the New Testament, as the creation stories begin the Old, not to answer the question "How?" but the question "Why?" "What can all this mean?" "Who was this man?" Like the prologue to St. John's Gospel, they are there to give an answer to theological, and not primarily to historical, questions.

Truly understood, that is their significance — and it never dates. But, alas, for millions today, so far from giving depth to the history, they merely tend to discredit it as history. These sorts of goings on, it is said, just don't happen — not in the real world. They simply transfer the whole thing into a fairy-tale world, where shepherds and stars get intertwined with reindeer and tinsel. And so we have the interval of artistic unreality, of angel chimes and Christmas trees, before the Stock Exchange takes over again on Monday morning — and the rupee drops another point and a further load of food is dumped into the sea.

I believe that we may have to do a rescue operation on Christmas not simply from commercialism — which ironically gives it one of its few points of contact with the modern world — but from the very artistry that is meant to show its truth. We may, for the time being, have to strip it down, to demythologize, not because we don't believe but precisely so that we can.

Let me put it this way. Is Christ unique because he is normal or because he is abnormal? The Gospel as I understand it, is that in this man we see the uniquely normal human being, the one who alone was what all of us are meant to be, the man who is uniquely free for others and free from self. That I believe is what the Evangelists are saying. But modern man would never guess it. Because of the language, the pictures, that they use, Jesus *appears* to be presented as though he were unique because he is abnormal. And that is no gospel — no good news to us — at all. A story like the Virgin Birth, for instance, is told by the men of the New Testament to enhance the significance of his humanity — to stress the fantastic truth that here was a man whose whole life, from birth to death, was lived not of the will of the flesh nor of the will of man but of God. But in fact for most people today it threatens to diminish his humanity. Such things are so unlike our mortal experiences that they cut him off — he cannot really be one of us at all: at most he is someone *like* us. And this is heresy, comparable with the ancient heresy that he wasn't really God but only like God. And of the two heresies it is today much the more destructive of faith. For unless he is really one of us, unless he is the truth about *our* humanity, the Gospel just cannot get started — never mind where it ends. The majority of men today cannot bear, cannot even hear, what Jesus represents because it appears so unlike their mortal experiences. And the Good News is simply not being preached until men are unable to bear it because it is so like.

Somehow we have got to let that get through — and to do so I should be prepared (for as long as it is necessary) to strip down everything. That for me is what that Christmas card succeeded in doing. When I looked at it, I said, "Yes, this is it. This is real, this is God for me." And what St. Paul called "my desire for my own flesh," my yearning for those bound up with me in the same humanity and generation, is simply that they may see it too — and find in that reality the focus of their commitment and the meaning of their lives.

To this end the Church exists to be "the sign of the Son of Man" to this and every generation. Men will grasp this reality and it will grasp them, not because they see it in the black and white of a Christmas card (though that can act as a pointer) but because they see it in the Son of Man on earth, in our flesh and blood. And when men do see such a sign, many respond — just as many always speak against it. God has raised up some notable signs for our generation. When one of them — Martin Luther King — passed through London recently, I am told that eight thousand people tried to hear him in St. Paul's. Another is Father Borelli, who has become a sign, a parable of hope, for the urchins of Naples.

I mention him particularly because, about the time when I received the Christmas card, I was asked to go out to supper in a fashionable part of London. At it was the twenty-year-old daughter of the house, who had come up specially for the occasion from a provincial university. She was glamorous, intelligent, and in love. But as soon as her university course was over and before doing anything else with her life, she had set herself to go out and live in the slums of Bombay to help with Father Borelli's work there. This, for her, was what "God" meant. She would have found it difficult to say the creeds, to accept most of the traditional formulations, images or stories. But this was for her *real:* this was the incarnation of God she could see. And an ounce of that reality is worth all the "magic" of Christmas put together.

CHAPTER 16
ASCENDANCY

What is a modern Christian to make of the Ascension story? It is a good test case of our ability to cope with the strange language, the antique cosmology, of which the Bible is full. Is this something that we can only discard? Or is it something we can transpose and use and fill with contemporary significance?

The story of the Ascension as recorded in Acts is a particularly clear-cut instance. In some ways it sticks out like a sore thumb. It uses the language of "up there" as naively as any passage in the New Testament. It forces us to ask what we make of it. Just what do we really believe the story is about? What was or is the Ascension?

First of all, two things which I believe it is *not*. And I stress these solely because it is important to liberate it for what it *is* from beneath misconceptions that overlay it and well-nigh smother it for many today.

It is not an account of a *movement in space*. And in this space age it is particularly necessary to make it clear that we don't believe this. So much Christian propaganda is prepared to cash in on confusion in people's minds.

Here is a rather crude example, from an advertisement for Bible-reading notes:

Entering a barrack room, the Scripture Reader found a number of soldiers conversing about spacemen. One soldier asked the name of the first man sent into orbit. Joining the conversation, the Scripture Reader said that he knew the names of two men who had gone into space before the birth of Christ. "Oh, no," said one of the men, "I can't believe that." Opening his Bible the Scripture Reader read out two references to Enoch and Elijah and then spoke of the ascension of the Lord Jesus Christ. As the men listened intently, the way of salvation was explained to them.

You may smile. But many intelligent people outside the Church really do suppose that this is the Christian line. And I fear there is much to encourage them, and that not only from fundamentalist sources. Here, for instance, is a comment from a book review by J. B. Phillips. Now I admire Phillips' translation of the New Testament greatly, but on the subject of the Ascension he complained of the author: "He appears reluctant to accept the story as a literal fact in history and I cannot think why." And he went on to quote in approval a remark by C. S. Lewis: "How else could a physical tangible body leave the surface of this planet?" I would like to stop and ask him (unhappily we can't ask Lewis): "Do you then really think it went on through space, passing out of the gravitational pull, first of the earth, then of the sun, and that now after two thousand light-years it is somewhere in the middle of the milky way?" Of course he doesn't. No one does. And yet there would be many intelligent Christians who would be shocked if you said that "he ascended into heaven" was not a literal statement. This only shows how lazy much of our thinking is. Indeed, I suspect many of us, if we were honest, try to have it both ways, and suppose that Jesus did literally go up in front of his disciples' eyes but that directly he got out of sight it somehow ceased to be a physical event at all, and the thing was called off!

But let us not probe. Let us come clean and say boldly that the Ascension is not a movement in space at all. The difference between Colonel Glenn and Jesus Christ is not that one came back while the other shot on. The doctrine of the Ascension is not that Jesus was the first astronaut — or even, on the Scripture Reader's reckoning, the third. It has nothing to do with such ideas at all, and the sooner we dissociate it from them, firmly and cleanly, the better the chances for the Christian Gospel in a twentieth-century scientific society.

Then, secondly, I believe it is important to say that it's not describing a *moment in time*. We have all been brought up to the idea that the Ascension is a separate historical event which "happened" forty days after Easter. But a study of the New Testament shows that this is entirely St. Luke's construction. Indeed, it is only in Acts that we find the familiar scheme: the Resurrection, followed forty days later by the Ascension, and ten days after that by the gift of the Spirit. In St. John all three take place on Easter Day and are part of a single complex. In fact, right through the rest of the New Testament (including St. Luke's own Gospel) and well on after it, until the Book of Acts becomes regarded as Scripture, the exaltation of Jesus is regularly linked with Easter. The resurrection appearances are of a Christ who, as he says on the Emmaus road, has already "entered into his glory." What the author of Acts has done in his teaching wisdom (and he is the father of the Christian year) is to say: "This great explosion of truth is too much to take in on one day — as it obviously was also for the disciples. So he pegs out the different aspects of it along a line of time, placing one after three days, another after the symbolic Biblical interval of forty days, attaching yet another to the liturgical feast of Pentecost. And the Ascension truth, that Jesus is not only living but Lord, he connects with the last of the resurrection visions. Very likely it finally dawned for some of the disciples then.

But the Ascension itself is not an "event," a moment in time, any more than it is a movement in space. As John Middleton Murry put it in one of his lay sermons: "Forty days is the period of a timeless spiritual happening. And such a timeless spiritual happening is what is indicated . . . by the forty days between Jesus' resurrection and ascension. It is the period in which it was realized that Jesus had . . . become a necessary part of the true idea of God." Christ henceforth is a *necessary part of the true idea of God*. That is the truth of the Ascension. The story of his going into heaven is simply a vivid way of saying in picture language, "Yes, that is where he belongs."

And this brings me, thirdly, to what the Ascension *is*. It is quite simply the assertion of Christ's ascendancy, of his claim to control the entire universe. That's why the Ascension has been called the most political of all Christian doctrines. It makes tremendous claims about the control of this world. As a child I used to think that the Ascension was the point at which the Christian faith became airborne and lost touch with this world altogether. It's true that the picture which the Ascension *story* conjures up is of motion from, the idea of going away. But whenever the Ascension of Christ is mentioned subsequently in the New Testament, the emphasis is always to be found not on the word "away" but on the word "over," on Jesus now being on top, in complete control. "He ascended far above all the heavens, that he might fill all things." "All authority has been given unto me in heaven and on earth." "Wherefore, God also hath highly exalted him, and given him a name which is above every name; that at the name of Jesus every knee should bow, of things in heaven, and things on earth, and things under the earth."

The doctrine of the Ascension is the assertion of the absolute sovereignty of Jesus Christ over every part of this universe, the crowning of the cross, the manifest triumph of his way of love over every other force in the world. "Christ is on the right hand of God," which means in modern language that he lives and rules in all the might and right of God himself. "Angels and authorities and powers have been made subject to him." That is to say, as a result of the Ascension, everything that has domination over the lives of men is ultimately in Christ's hands, including all the mysterious forces that appear to have our world in their grip, that drive us into wars that nobody wants, that plunge us willy-nilly into economic crises, and bring us to the brink of racial suicide. All the ideologies and -isms and economic bogies, the dark surging forces which work below the surface of our conscious lives, which possess men in crowds, and set class against class, black against white — these are the angels, authorities, and powers of our modern world. Whether we prefer to picture them as personal or impersonal, these are the things we all recognize as determining the course of history and enslaving the minds and bodies of men. The affirmation of the Ascension is that Christ really is in control of these things even when we are not, that there is no depth which his victory has not affected, no department of life in which his authority does not and must not run.

Everything that reduces more of this world — this sordid, material world of which God has chosen to be the God — to the sovereignty of Christ is a proclamation of the Gospel, an announcement to the world that Christ is in it and reigns over it. Anything — however pious and spiritual — that in fact leaves other forces in control of everyday life is a denial of the Gospel, an announcement to the world that Christ is absent from it. Ascension Day is the yearly reminder to the world of the sentence which has been served on it — that of the utter reduction, the unconditional surrender, of every principality and authority and power in it to the love and the holiness and the righteousness of Jesus Christ. Ascension Day is also the yearly reminder to the Church of its function in the world — namely, that of bringing all men and every department of life under the obedience of Christ.

The doctrine of the Ascension is not a fairy story from the pre-space age. It's the claim — if we can set it free to speak — that everything (even space travel itself) must be subjected to the priorities of Christ. For he reigns in the might and right of God.

CHAPTER **17**

THE HOLY
SPIRIT

"We have not even heard that there is a Holy Spirit" (Acts 19:2). That is not literally true. Everyone in this country has heard of the Holy Spirit. But in a deeper sense it is profoundly true. People have not "heard" in any way that has gotten through. They have no idea on the pulses of their experience of the reality that is being talked about — and that goes for many so-called disciples, too, such as were these people at Ephesus. The Holy Spirit is supremely "the unknown God," the God-shaped blank of our day. In fact for most people he is a shapeless blank — for the images in which the Church has sought to make the Spirit real and vivid to the imagination correspond to nothing in their minds. There is a story of a puzzled Japanese trying to get a grasp of Christianity: "The Father I know, the Son I know, but who is this Holy Bird?" The very word Ghost we use of him tells its tale. He is a phantom: people simply don't know what we're talking about.

One of the complaints I had about *Honest to God* was that I left out of it any mention of the Spirit. This is in fact not true, as I referred at some length to St. Paul's profound language about the Spirit in Romans 8 — the greatest passage on it in the whole New Testament. True, I didn't use the *word* much (just as I'd be prepared, if necessary, to drop the word God — if there was another). But in another sense the whole book was about the Spirit — and people did not recognize it. For the Spirit is pre-eminently the aspect of the reality of God I was trying to bring home. He is the very ground of our being, nearer to us than our own selves, the beyond *in the midst*. He is God at hand — at ground-floor level — the way into the divine.

So often in our teaching, as in our creeds, we start at the other end — beginning, expansively, with God the Father Almighty, working through to the Son (about whom naturally we can say a good deal), and then rather petering out when we come to the Spirit. But the New Testament insists on the opposite approach. We come to the Father only through the Son, and we can know the Son only in the Spirit. And this surely is constantly verified in experience. Most people I have watched coming to a living faith have first found themselves drawn into the fellowship of the Spirit as a dynamic transforming reality. From that they come to see Jesus in a very different light. And then, perhaps much later, they begin to grasp how this world could possibly make sense in terms of an overarching Fatherly purpose.

The Holy Spirit is the window into everything that God in Christ means. But, as George Herbert said,

A man who looks on glass
On it may stay his eye.

And the trouble with the Holy Spirit begins when we stay our eye and try to define or describe the glass for its own sake. And, of course, we can't, for in itself it is an invisible medium. To help us, the Church has tried engraving images on the glass to focus our attention and imagination. But, whatever help these may have been, I suspect that today they are more of a distraction. Indeed, if it is at all true that "our image of God must go," it is doubly true that our image of the Spirit must go. For the traditional ones with which we have worked are now, I believe, a positive hindrance.

There are two main types of image that have been used of the Spirit.

The first arises when we transpose this intensely personal, or rather interpersonal, reality into the mental image of *a* Person, a separate Individual. But classical Christian theology, when it spoke of the Spirit as a Person, never intended this: the "Persons" of the doctrine of the Trinity were not personalities in our modern sense. The result is that most people's doctrine of the Trinity is in fact tritheistic, and they imagine God as three persons on the end of three telephone lines with each of whom they can talk and do business. And as a Person the Holy Spirit seems to have no form or content. It's difficult even to imagine him as a man, in the way that is possible with Christ or the Father. The traditional visual aid is a dove, and that doesn't help very much.

Sometimes the Bible speaks of the reality of Holy Spirit in terms of "he" and sometimes in terms of "it" — and so, quite naturally, do we. The trouble is that both our corresponding images, of a Person and a Thing, are calamitous. That of the Spirit as a Person, as I have just said, simply succeeds in making him unreal — we can't even envisage him as a human being. But the second image of the Spirit, as a sort of impersonal substance, of which one receives gifts or doses, is even more disastrous.

This underlies the popular conception, for instance, of the gift of the Spirit at confirmation. At baptism, people think, you get a sort of spiritual inoculation. Then confirmation comes along as a booster injection to give you the extra you need for a grown-up life. With some people this "takes" and they stick. With others it doesn't, they feel no difference, and they reckon they can't be the religious type. What a ghastly misunderstanding of the whole Biblical reality of life in the Spirit! No wonder people don't recognize the Spirit. No wonder they feel they have missed out on this whole element in Christianity.

The basic defect of both of these images is that they are entirely individualistic — whereas the distinctive thing about the New Testament, in contrast with the Old, is not that the Spirit is now a Person as opposed to a Thing (both personal and impersonal language continue to be used), but that the Spirit is now a corporate reality, a shared possession of the whole people of God. In the Old Testament the Spirit of God came only upon certain outstanding individuals, prophets, kings, craftsmen, etc. In the New Testament all the Lord's people are prophets: the Spirit is poured out on every Tom, Dick, and Harry. It belongs to the whole Body of Christ and to every individual by virtue of his membership to it. The *koinonia,* or common ownership, of Holy Spirit was the distinctive, thrilling, announcement of the new age. It was the great new fact that made the apostolic Church the infectious, dynamic, captivating reality it was.

The first prerequisite therefore of any Christian image of the Spirit is that it should primarily be corporate. This, I believe, is the great contribution of the section on the Spirit in T. O. Wedel's book, *The Coming Great*

Church.[1] He draws out in a masterly way the analogy of the corporate spirit experienced in many ordinary human relationships, for instance, in the esprit de corps of a great college or team. Those who have read it will remember the vivid passage about sedate professors being moved to speak with tongues at a football game, uttering words they later disavowed! Such a spirit takes people out of themselves and binds them together in one body. It creates a sense of belongingness and inspires them to things they could never have done on their own.

Canon Wedel is the first to say that it is an inadequate image; but I am sure it starts at the right place and it takes us a long way. Of course the Holy Spirit is much more than anything generated by a crowd. In fact the significance of the Biblical word holy is precisely "with a difference." God is Father, but with a difference — therefore Jesus instinctively addresses him as "holy Father." God is Spirit, but with a profound difference from anything known in a purely human fellowship — and therefore "holy Spirit." Yet there is an equally profound affinity. As the book of Proverbs puts it, in a beautiful image, "The spirit of man is the candle of the Lord." The Holy Spirit is the point at which the spirit, the depth, of our lives, individually and corporately, is met and touched by the fire of the living God.

For the Christian, this holy Spirit of God is given definition and embodiment as the Spirit of Christ in the fellowship of the Church. It is defined by it, but not confined to it. This is where men should be able to recognize the Spirit for what it most truly is. This does not mean that it is something peculiarly religious or distinctively churchy. For wherever the mystery of life runs out into

[1] S.C.M. Press, London, 1947, pp. 56–65.

the truth of God or human relationships are caught up into his creative or recreative power, there is the Holy Spirit.

The Christian is aware of the Spirit as the encompassing gracious reality to which his life lies open at every point. For the humanist, life is simply what you make of it. For the Christian, life is response, openness, obedience to the movement and the moment of the Spirit. The Church, the fellowship of Holy Spirit, is called to be the sacrament of that movement and that moment — making it all visible and tangible. And this sacramental fellowship, this holy community, finds its focus in the weekly act, at which it comes together to be renewed in the one Spirit of the one Body. This is the quick center of everything Christians are and do. God forbid that anyone who comes into contact with *this* Body should ever be able to say those chilling words: "We have not even heard that there is a Holy Spirit."

CHAPTER 18
THE TRINITY

I was once asked a question after one of my talks: "How would you teach a child the doctrine of the Trinity?" It was one of the easiest questions I have received. The answer was "I wouldn't."

The question pinpoints very well what has happened to the Christian faith and what has come over this doctrine in particular.

Is there anyone whose heart does not sink a bit as Trinity Sunday comes round year by year? Certainly this must be true of preachers and I am sure it is true of most laymen. Just what is this of which we are supposed to make sense? "The Father incomprehensible, the Son incomprehensible, the Holy Ghost incomprehensible," says the Athanasian Creed. "The whole lot incomprehensible," says the ordinary man. How on earth have we got stuck with this abracadabra as the heart of the Christian faith?

"Firmly I believe and truly," the hymn tells us to sing, "God is three and God is one." And we dutifully chant it. But what really does it *mean*? The essence of Christianity seems to have boiled down to a formula, as arid and unintelligible as $E = MC^2$ that Einstein told us was the clue to the physical universe. And the Church has even invented a festival to celebrate this formula. It was popularized by an Englishman, St. Thomas à Becket, Archbishop of Canterbury, and the Church of England has gone to the length of numbering the remaining Sundays of the Christian year after this made-up festival and not after the Biblical feast of Pentecost, like the rest of Christendom.

In fact the whole thing has got out of proportion. Originally the doctrine was created to describe, define, and safeguard an experience. But in the process the experience seems to have drained right out of it, the dogma has become airborne, and we are asked if we believe in the formula as though this were what being a Christian means. We are left with a shell on our hands from which the life that shaped it has long since departed.

In this situation there are two things we can do. We can start from the shell, the doctrine, and try to fill it again with new life. And this is presumably what my questioner wanted me to do for his hypothetical child. And this is in fact what traditional Christian education has attempted to do. It spells out the various doctrines of the Faith, so that the child has a framework within which to fit the experience of the Christian life when and as it becomes real for him. It provides him with the formula ahead of the experience; it gives him the answer before he has worked out the sum. And this is what we have called religious instruction. Its presupposition is the one underlying the Catechism, namely that the Church supplies in prefabricated form the answers to the questions it itself asks.

But this whole approach is I believe becoming increasingly hollow to a generation whose search for truth in every other field begins from precisely the opposite end. "A church that goes on *dictating truths* rather than sitting with the people and working out the real questions is certainly not living in solidarity with the men of today." Those words come from a young Dutch theologian out of his experience of young people's work at the World Council of Churches. And he goes on:

I am not suggesting that there are no truths, or that the Church does not know them. I only suggest that modern people do not understand *given truths.* . . . Therefore, religious instruction cannot be given with a simple catechism book any longer. The question-and-answer period has to be replaced by the question-after-question period, in which the answer may be found, the question may disappear, or the questions may stand unanswered. Until now, the authority concept of most of our churches has been imposed; we talk because we know. And we hardly know how painful this is to those who listen to us.[1]

I am sure he is right. The approach to truth for our generation starts from life rather than dogma. To require the doctrine in advance of the experience it is meant to be defining is to ask for it to be rejected — not only because it is a shell with nothing inside, but because it gives the impression that the results are prescribed. Theology is dismissed because people cannot believe that it is a genuine search for the truth. It appears to the outsider like a closed debate of mandarins within the agreed terms of their own system. And the doctrine of the Trinity would seem to most people the supreme example of such closed-circuit thinking. Start from it and there seems no path back into ordinary experience, no point at which

1 Albert van den Heuvel, *The Humiliation of the Church* (S.C.M. Press, London, 1967), p. 59.

its truth could conceivably be tested by reference to everyday relationships with other people and things.

I believe there is an urgent need to begin again from the other end. For theology, as I understand it, is not about heavenly entities beyond our ken. It is about ordinary experience, in depth, at the level of ultimate concern. It is describing the realities by which we are surrounded, the relationships in which we find ourselves, when we look at them not simply at the superficial level at which we spend most of our time, but when we ask what is most deeply true about the universe in which we live. The Christian affirmation is that beyond all the contradictions and tragedies of life there are certain realities from which finally we cannot get away and which will not let us go. These are realities which can meet us, if we are open to them, as the depth and ground of all our relationships, speaking to us of a truth, a way, and a life that can give coherence and meaning to everything in our experience.

And these are the realities which the doctrine of the Trinity attempts to coordinate and hold together — namely, "the grace of our Lord Jesus Christ, the love of God, and the fellowship of the Holy Spirit."

First, the love of God — the conviction that deep down, beyond the power of anything else to destroy or to separate, the undergirding reality in life, the final relationship for which we are made and in which we are held, is not to be described simply in terms of an invariable mathematical regularity but in terms of an utterly trustworthy personal reliability. "Abba, Father" — that for Jesus was the reality in which his whole life was grounded. And the Christian affirmation is that this is ultimate, this is God.

But for the Christian Jesus does not simply point away from himself to this Fatherly reality of love. He embodies it. In the grace of our Lord Jesus Christ the Christian knows something which speaks supremely, in terms of flesh and blood, of who God is, and what this love has done and can do. He defines it as no one else can. In this human life and death, says the Christian, we see not simply a man living close to God; we see God exposed, God in action as sheer grace, accepting the unacceptable, reconciling the world to himself.

And it does not end there. In the fellowship of Holy Spirit the Christian finds himself partaking in a shared reality which again transcends anything this world can give or take away. To say that this is just a human fellowship is to fly in the face of the facts as much as to say that Jesus was just a good man. For in this the Christian discovers himself caught up in a life and a power which goes beyond anything that one human being can offer to another. Here once more he strikes that depth of reality which he can only indicate by the word God.

Here then are three relationships which take him through to what is most ultimate and unassailable. He cannot deny the same quality to any of them; they are all for him "God." Yet palpably they speak of one reality, not three.

And it is this unity and diversity of the Christian experience which the doctrine of the Trinity was designed to affirm and safeguard. To do this adequately the theologians, the scientists of the Church, found themselves forced to a more and more complex formula, although it also has the beauty and simplicity of Einstein's equation for describing the truth of the physical universe. *But the ordinary man can live life without either.*

Introducing a child or indeed an adult to the Trinity is not teaching him the doctrine, instructing him in the formula, which he will probably find as alarming and confusing as I, as a layman, find most scientific formulae. Rather, it is making it possible for him to know the reality on the pulses of his experience, to discover it as the ground and power of his whole being. It is in the first place a question of spiritual education rather than religious instruction — of entering into a shared life of which this is the most fundamental experience. Then perhaps — maybe a long time afterwards — the definition will be seen to have some meaning, because there is something to define.

CHAPTER 19
ANGELS

New Christian, that *enfant terrible* of Christian journalism in Britain, celebrated its first anniversary with an editorial saying that the time has come when angels may go: "Their removal from the pulpits, the Sunday School lessons and the liturgies would surely be a real gain." It provoked more correspondence than any other article.

Yet, if we are honest, there's a large part of each one of us which must surely echo that sentiment. For most ordinary people angels merely add to the cocoon of fantasy and unreality in which the Christian Gospel is wrapped. So far from making the Faith more real, they undoubtedly make it more unreal, remote, and airborne. I simply do not see how this can be denied. Insofar, therefore, as one is trying to start from where people are, and make the Christian faith meaningful in terms of what is real to them, I agree with *New Christian.*

Having said that, I suggest we have a look at what's happened and see whether, starting from the Church's end (which is not the same thing at all), it's possible to interpret what belief in angels is really about. For it is a belief that is *meant* to add to, rather than detract from, the reality and richness of life. If it doesn't, has something important been lost? And, if so, how can we restore it?

The story of our modern world is a story of the steady loss of reality suffered over the centuries by these ethereal beings.

In the Middle Ages everyone believed in angels, and took them desperately literally. In their odd moments, theologians, when they weren't arguing whether an archdeacon could be saved, spent their time disputing the number of angels that could dance on the point of a pin. Angelology was already on the way to being little more than an intellectual puzzle, a sort of medieval substitute for *The Times* crossword.

Later, with the Renaissance, angels became domesticated, and we find them appearing as cherubs — sweet little boys with wings, whose blissful smiles certainly bear little enough resemblance to their counterparts on earth.

Then, with the Romantic movement, they got sentimentalized as those sexless creatures who float through Pre-Raphaelite paintings and stained-glass windows.

By this time they had become so thoroughly vapid and meaningless that it's hardly surprising that most people have now dismissed them altogether. They've become part of the fantasy world, with fairies and Father Christmas. A survey would doubtless reveal more people prepared to believe in flying saucers than in angels. We have reached the end of the road.

What do we do now? The one thing I am sure we can't do is just to go on as if nothing had happened. I remember years ago when I was on the staff of a theological college listening to a Compline address on angels from a leading Anglo-Catholic vicar, with whom I have joked about it since. But at the time I was angry. Just because we were in chapel we were exposed to a devotional fundamentalism that could only conceivably survive unquestioned there, and which I felt was an assault on the young men's critical faculties. It simply took for granted these invisible denizens of space as medieval men had believed them.

Far be it from me to be dogmatic on the other side. In this age of constant fresh discoveries by radioastronomy no one's going to be so foolish as to *deny* what may be around the universe. But I cannot say too strongly that it is no part of the Christian Faith to put one's belief in hitherto unidentified flying objects. For believing in angels is not committing oneself to statements in the field of astrophysics any more than believing in Adam and Eve is committing oneself to statements in the field of anthropology. In neither case are we required to believe in the existence of actual beings who are or were around the world as we are. For angels are not literal entities that could be picked up on radar if we got their wavelength. Rather, like Adam and Eve, they are ways of representing or picturing certain convictions — theological convictions, not scientific convictions — about the meaning of life. They stand for the belief, if we may so put it, that there's always an inside to events, a personal as well as an impersonal aspect, a spiritual as well as a material, that the entire universe is shot through with God and his living activity. Whether angels are any longer the best or most helpful way of expressing this conviction is another matter. But let us try to understand it.

First, however, let's clear up one misunderstanding. For the men of the Bible angels were the communications system between God (who was in heaven) and men (who were on earth). Obviously for getting about they must be imagined as having wings — and in the visions of heaven in Isaiah or Ezekiel or the book of Revelation they are represented, in highly poetic imagery, as winged creatures. But when angels appear to men and women on earth there is nothing whatever to suggest that they *look* different from ordinary people. In fact they *are* ordinary people, either real or in dreams, who are seen at the time or subsequently as having something to say from God. The classic case of this is Abraham, who, according to the Epistle to the Hebrews, "entertained angels unawares." The three men for whom Abraham and Sarah cooked lunch were three men — and there is no suggestion in the story that they looked or were any different. They were afterwards (though not, interestingly enough, in the Genesis story) called "angels" because they were recognized as bringing a message from the Lord. If God was in an event, then the human agents or interpreters of it were seen as angels. For an angel is what an angel does.

We have the same usage in the phrase "be an angel," which doesn't mean "go and get yourself feathers" but "do something angelic." The Greek word *angellos* simply means a messenger. It is that used of John the Baptist, who was indeed a man sent from God; but certainly he didn't have feathers or wings. And St. Paul applies it to the Christian ministry. Sometimes indeed there is doubt whether a person should be described in terms of his physical aspect or of his angelic function and significance. Thus, in the earliest account of the empty tomb in Mark, we read that there was "a young man" sitting there in a "white robe." In Luke it has become "two men" in "dazzling apparel," and in Matthew an "angel" whose "appearance was like lightning and his raiment white as snow." I suggest that what the women actually *saw* was, as we should say today, a man in a white shirt. But what he had to say was seen as a message from God. So the event becomes written up in language that any first-century reader would instantly recognize as symbolic.

As I said, angels for the Bible stand for the conviction that within or behind all that happens there is a personal, a spiritual reality to be reckoned with. It is the Biblical way (or, rather a Biblical way) of denying a final materialism, the belief that everything can be explained by the outside of events, merely in terms of the physical and the impersonal. Expressions of this spiritual dimension to all reality are the angels of the nations in Daniel, the angels of the churches in Revelation, and the angels of children in Jesus' own words (Matt. 18:10).

Let me try to make real this spiritual dimension, what the Seer of Revelation vividly calls a "door opened into heaven," from three areas of experience.

1. There is the meaning of the whole process of nature and history. Consider this breathtaking scene from the Apocalypse (Rev. 5:11–14):

Then as I looked I heard the voice of countless angels. These were all around the throne and the living creatures and the elders. Myriads upon myriads there were, thousands upon thousands and they cried aloud: "Worthy is the Lamb, the Lamb that was slain, to receive all power and wealth, wisdom and might, honour and glory and praise!" Then I heard every created thing in heaven and on earth and under the earth and in the sea, all that is in them, crying: "Praise and honour, glory and might, to him who sits on the throne and to the Lamb for ever and ever!" And the four living creatures said, "Amen," and the elders fell down and worshipped.

What a stupendous vision of the entire created universe as one gigantic act of worship, as spiritual in its ultimate, inner significance. We shall indeed be impoverished if we cannot catch its thrill. It is this interpretation that the dimension of "angels and archangels and all the company of heaven" is intended to supply. Let us not write it off. It is what is conveyed in modern terms by the sweep of Teilhard de Chardin's *Phenomenon of Man* or more soberly and scientifically by Sir Alister Hardy's recent Gifford Lectures, "The Living Stream" and "The Divine Flame," though it is significant that neither of these think of mentioning angels.

2. There is the field that today is occupied by the powers lying beyond the threshold of conscious control, the ideologies and -isms that grip men in groups, the forces of the collective unconscious, the archetypes of Jung, the Shadow, the Censor, not to mention the highly mythological figures of Oedipus and Eros and Thanatos, or the ghoulish monsters of science fiction. No one doubts their psychological reality, and it doesn't take much imagination to translate the Biblical language of the world rulers of this darkness and the spiritual wickedness in high places, or the vision of Michael and his angels warring with the Devil and his angels, into analyses of race riots or the individual psyche. "The heights" and "the depths" of which St. Paul speaks in Romans 8 as powerless against the love of Christ are essential to the scope of the Christian understanding of man and the cosmos.

3. And then, at the more homely level, there is the conviction of God's constant presence in ordinary life. For the men of the Bible angels came in and out of everyday events entirely naturally. "An angel appeared to Joseph in a dream" means simply, as we should put it,

that Joseph had a dream in which he was told to get out quickly, and that in this he saw "the hand of God." Such incidents need not be miraculous interventions: simply ordinary events on their "inside." The way the men of the Bible registered that these weren't just accidents or coincidences was to talk of angels as we still talk of providence. *God* was at work wonderfully, graciously.

I am not suggesting that we try to make this dimension real for people by pressing upon them the language of angels. In that I agree with *New Christian*. For it will probably have precisely the opposite effect. But I do not want to throw out the reality or cut the lifeline of its connection with the Biblical imagery and myth. For this has great evocative power, which one day we may be able to accept as the poetry it is. Above all let's stop being so desperately prosaic and pedestrian about it all. Angels are a *jeu d'esprit*, part of the dance of life. And maybe if we cannot take them from the theologians we can still glimpse them through the words of the poets. So here, to end, is Francis Thompson:

> *The angels keep their ancient places;*
> *Turn but a stone, and start a wing!*
> *'Tis ye, 'tis your estranged faces,*
> *That miss the many-splendoured thing.*

CHAPTER 20
A TRULY REPRESENTATIVE MINISTRY

The Holy Bible and the Sacred Ministry — these have traditionally come together as means of grace, twin channels of Christ's coming, celebrated successively by the Church on the second and third Sundays in Advent.

Time was when it was possible to take a simple, uncomplicated, authoritarian view of each of these. The Bible simply came down from heaven, in the Authorized Version, some with Apocryphas and some without, and all one had to do was to accept it as the Word of God in a quite literal dictated sense and live by it. There has been a profound revolution. All intelligent people recognize that such a fundamentalism is no longer possible. Many feel not a little threatened and think that the bottom has been removed from their faith. And yet if we are prepared to go through the mill and the agonizing reappraisal a real revival and renewal becomes possible. And there has of late been a tremendous revival of Biblical scholarship, Biblical theology, and Bible study, reanimating all the Churches.

We are not so ready to acknowledge that we have an equally profound revolution on our hands with regard to the other channel of communication, the Sacred Ministry. It is no longer possible to take a simplistic, authoritarian view of the priest as a man sent from God, appearing as a young curate, ready fitted with a dog collar, from the other side of the line, to speak the things of God to a docile, listening laity. With the collapse of this fundamentalism, there is a danger of complete confusion and uncertainty about the ministry. The clergy themselves have been described as "the puzzled profession," and the laity are still more at sea.

This is partly a social, partly a theological revolution (just as the critique of Biblical fundamentalism was partly historical — it simply could not be squared with the facts — and partly theological — verbally guaranteed infallible propositions are not the way the God disclosed in the Bible reveals himself anyhow). In the case of the ministry, it is partly that the role of the priest in a secular society has become acutely problematic, with the traditional openings in which he operated fast being filled in by the welfare state. But more fundamentally, the recovery of a true understanding of the ministry as belonging to the whole Body of Christ rather than to a clerical club makes many question the distinctive role of the clergy. There is hardly a clerical or lay gathering I attend where this is not the unexpressed question beneath the surface.

It is urgent that we grasp this problem positively. The revolution, as in the case of the Bible, is not a threat when properly understood. On the contrary, it is full of creative and liberating possibilities. But if we are to seize them we must get our theology right and whole.

Our minds are cluttered up with all sorts of false presuppositions. People still talk of ordination — rather than baptism — as "going into the Church." Or, if they are not as ignorant as that, they speak of it as "going into the ministry." But that is in fact a better description of confirmation. Indeed, the late Bishop George Bell of Chichester once suggested that the wording of the confirmation service should run: "Take thou authority to exercise the ministry of a layman in the Church of God." But if this is true, how is the ordained ministry related to the ministry which belongs to all God's people? I think we have got to be careful as to how we answer that question.

First of all there is an important distinction to be drawn between the Old Testament and the New. The Old Testament priesthood was vicarious, in the sense that it did what the rest of the people could not do. It mediated between them and God. There was one tribe in Israel — the tribe of Levi — which was priestly and eleven that were not. But in the New Testament the whole structure is abolished. Christ is the only Mediator between men and God and the sole High Priest. In the new Israel there is no priestly caste or tribe. The whole Body of Christ is a priestly body and every member of it by virtue of his baptism has his share in the royal priesthood of the Master. The ordained ministry is not vicarious, to do what the others cannot do, but representative, commissioned to exercise in the name of the Body the ministry which belongs to every member. The ordained man is given formal authority to preach and proclaim in the name of the Church what every member should be preaching and proclaiming. He is given formal authority to exercise the ministry of reconciliation and forgiveness which belongs by right to every member of the Church as the healing community. He is given formal authority to lead and preside at the celebration which is the concelebration of the whole people of God — for every celebration of the Holy Communion is a lay celebration, by the whole *laos,* of which the bishop or presbyter is not the celebrant but, as the early Church always called him, the president.

In other words, if we ask what is distinctive about the ordained ministry we don't get the truest, deepest answer in terms of what the others cannot do. Of course, there are things which by the Church's discipline and order certain of its officers are given authority to do. But these vary — the rite of confirmation, for example, has been very variously delegated in different ages and communions of the Church. In any case, these particular functions are all ones which the Church itself sets them apart to perform in its name. The ministry they exercise is the ministry of the whole Body — not of the Body apart from the Head (as if their authority came merely from below), nor of the Head apart from the Body, but of the Head working through the Body. It is a representative ministry of and to the whole people of God.

And it is in consequence of this that theirs is such a key place and crucial responsibility. Precisely because it is a *representative* ministry, the level of ministry in the Church will seldom in practice rise much above the level of the ordained ministry. That is why its quality is even more important than its quantity. We hear much about the shortage of priests — and as a bishop I see as much as anyone of the tragic loss of opportunities because we simply have not got the manpower. No one needs to persuade me of this. And yet I constantly wonder whether we do not ordain too many people. I am sure we baptize too many people. I have no doubt that I confirm too many people (judging by the subsequent wastage); and I suspect that we ordain too many people. For the longer I go on in this job the more convinced I become that bad priests are worse than no priests. The ordained ministry is the channel — or the bottleneck — through which the ministry of Christ is communicated to his people and through them to the world. That is what the Church says to a man at ordination: "You are to be that channel — or that bottleneck." Thank heaven when the channels become blocked or furred up the Spirit of God finds other ways — but we neglect these channels at our peril.

It is good to be forced to look again at our channels of communication. What sort of channels are we seeking to construct? There was a time when it was possible to think of the ordained ministry as a sort of pipeline over the head of the Church by which grace was transmitted from Christ to his people, and the important thing was to see that there were no breaks in the succession and that the supply remained pure and undefiled from the world. But it ran, down through the centuries, out of any creative relationship to the laity, and any suggestion that the laity might have a real ministry was seen as a threat to the professional clergy, or as an attempt to bypass the sole sufficiency of the authorized means of grace. Such a view is as impossible today as the corresponding view of the Bible — but psychologically it has left its hangover. And as long as we cherish a vicarious conception of the priesthood (where the priest is there to do what the people can't), then every extension of lay ministry will seem to be gained at the expense of what before was the prerogative of the clergy. It is no wonder that under the surface there is so much mistrust.

But once we can wholeheartedly embrace a truly representative conception of the ordained ministry — with the priest as the *persona,* the commissioned representative in the name of the Head, of the whole people of God — then his ministry expands with theirs. He is released (as one knows in one's own experience) from the confines of a professional caste to become what Christ his Master was, the true layman because he is the true priest. He is called — and what a call it is — to be the truest representative of the *laos,* of the Son of Man on earth, the servant of the servants of God (to use the fine title of the Pope). In this he must stand where his Lord stood, not less of a man but more of a man, not less open to the world but more open. Teilhard de Chardin got it when he wrote: "To the full extent of my power because I am a priest I wish from now on to be the *first* to become conscious of all that the world loves, pursues and suffers; I want to be the *first* to seek, to sympathize and to suffer; the *first* to open myself out and sacrifice myself — to become more widely human and more nobly of the earth than any of the world's servants." That is the call of the priesthood — to be the open channel of incarnation, of suffering and of glory, to be the representative man, on behalf of Christ and his people. If that channel can be kept wide open — as wide open as God's love for the world — then indeed it can still, as powerfully as in any past age, be a means of Christ's coming and a sacrament of his presence.

CHAPTER 21
MINISTRY IN THE MELTING

"When are you going to send us another curate?" The answer, if the bishop is honest, is increasingly likely to be "Never."

I sat through a day recently listening to theological college principals and representatives of their governing bodies discussing the implications of the 30 percent drop in a single year of candidates recommended for training for ordination in the Church of England. The prevailing atmosphere was that we were bound to be "optimistic," step up recruiting, and plan on the assumption that this was merely a "trough." It was lack of faith to believe that it represented a permanent trend.

Of course, no one can be sure. I personally suspect that this is the writing on the wall, and that the statistics are symptomatic of much deeper and wider forces. But I am not for that reason pessimistic.

On the contrary, in contrast with what one has seen, for instance, in Sweden or large parts of the United States, where nothing looks like toppling the traditional structures however irrelevant, the great, and unexpected, hope is the rapidity in England with which the old is dissolving. Indeed, if it were not for the injection of vast sums from the Church Commissioners, our inherited system, with its thousands of consecrated buildings and beneficed clergy, would in many areas have collapsed long since.

The shortage of men and money from the parishes now puts a big question mark against the whole future. But if we act only because we are forced to from economic motives we shall merely prove the Marxists right and derive no spiritual benefit from it. The source of hope is that even in situations of relative strength many of our most intelligent ordinands, clergy and laity, are rebelling against a system which, they feel, condemns the church to the periphery of the modern world and its ministry to what Gibson Winter calls "residential chaplaincies to family life." Here, for instance, is a typical letter I have just received from the vicar of an inner suburban parish:

For some time I have been one of those seriously troubled by the pattern of the full-time paid parish ministry, and the way in which this has been a major factor in allowing the Christian witness to be a pool in a backwater instead of part of the main stream of the life of the community.

Various streams of thought and experience have converged to bring me to the point at which I have to ask myself whether I can spend the rest of my life operating a system which, in certain respects, may be a definite hindrance to the Kingdom.

I should be most grateful if I could come and talk about these matters with you — not in terms of escape from the parochial situation, but of possible experiments and developments.

In discussion, he told me that he felt himself in an increasingly false position as a professional, paid to mind the pool and keep it full. He wanted to explore the possibility of taking a year to complete the necessary qualifications and then of teaching in a comprehensive school *while remaining vicar*. As he said, this was by no means in order to "escape from the parochial situation." It was to crack open the professional line which is at the moment restricting ministry within the Body of Christ to those on one side of it.

The corollary of this approach was not to say to the bishop, "When are you going to send us another curate?" (though in the *present* situation, with clergy ordained without a trade and with an absence of any real lay ministry, it may be essential for the present curate to stay on while his vicar trains). Its corollary, rather, was to say to the local church, "This is a corporate decision. I can only consider it if you too are prepared to train to 'enter the ministry.'"

What this involves can, I believe, only be discovered by trying. One would have to start by asking what Christian ministry in and to "the main stream of life" in that community really means; what are the needs, what are the skills and resources available, what are the insights, technical and theological, that would have to be acquired. It may result in groups and courses for many different things — most, including those in adult lay theology, properly provided not by the church but by the local authority.

There would be no firm line between those training for the priesthood and for any other kind of ministry — only a variety of different specialisms. The Apostolic function is not the paternalistic one of "sending curates" but of saying, as in Acts 6: "Look out from among you men of good repute whom we may appoint." And the primary responsibility of the diocese must be to organize the training and care of what in the future must, I am convinced, be the *main* ministry of the local church. There will of course continue to be an essential place for the man, ordained or lay, released for full-time ministry, residential or functional, on the payroll of the church; but such financial support cannot be taken for granted, as it is at the moment, in the act of ordination. Above all there will remain a need, and a growing need, for theological specialists, male and female, for whom our colleges of theology (fewer and larger, and for the most part around university centers) must continue to cater. (Is there, incidentally, any case for separate colleges for men and women — or indeed for councils or boards of *women's* ministry?)

It is because I see this as a much more relevant pattern that I welcome the creaks in the present system, painful though the process is. But if reform is not to be stultified at least two other things have got to give.

The first is the mystique of character and indelibility with which since the Middle Ages "holy" orders have been surrounded and isolated. Ours is an age which thinks in functional terms. As John Taylor put it in the *Church Missionary Society News Letter:*[1]

An *ad hoc* response is the only kind of obedience which rings true to many of the liveliest young Christians to-day. They will give themselves to meet a need without reserve but also without pretensions. They will serve but without a label. A call makes sense to them but not a vocation. The only response they can make with integrity is "I will go now. . . How can I tell what the opening will be after that?"

And if this should seem a peculiarly Protestant view of the ministry, I would add this from the notable article

[1] January, 1966.

on "Priesthood and Paternalism" by Terry Eagleton in *New Blackfriars*,[2] the organ of the English Dominicans:

It seems to me that we may have to return to the sense of the priest's role as much less permanent and much more intermittent: the priest is the man who has received authority to celebrate the liturgy for the people. Why this involves wearing a black suit and being celibate and spending his time between liturgical activities in generally fostering Christian welfare seems to me much less obvious. I don't think we will ever have a really non-paternalist church until priests (and I think the word "priest" has to go, as well as the word "minister" which again suggests a kind of specific relationship) are ordinary workers with families who have this special function to celebrate the liturgy within a church where the activities of teaching, welfare and preaching are genuinely common, and not the monopoly of a caste.

Why should not men (and of course eventually women) be ordained Breakers of Bread on the same basis that Presbyterians ordain Elders and Anglicans admit Readers? The initial solemn act is never repeated, but they can exercise their ministry only as and where they are called and licensed to do so.

The second blockage consists in the whole system of which the Church Commissioners are the curators, though not the originating cause. (They are not personally to blame, and where indeed they have the initiative, e.g., in the stewardship of the Church's endowments, they deserve on the whole nothing but praise.)

Let me put it this way. Apart from the oversight of training and care, the chief contribution of the diocese in the future is likely not to be grants for stipends and buildings — at least on nothing like the present all-con-

2 December, 1965.

suming scale. In the inner-city areas at any rate (where the next ten years will see the real crunch), I trust we shall be relieved of mountains of masonry that at present diverts almost all energy from mission to maintenance. And we shall have to operate with fewer full-time clergy grouped around fewer historic parish churches. But in between there will be an almost unlimited need for housing (including, where they are needed, meeting rooms for house-churches) for community-leaders ordained and lay, from which Christians may exercise their ministry in and to the neighborhood. The greatest help the diocese can give to a downtown area is likely to consist in the provision, through its own housing association, of accommodation at a reasonable rent for priest-workers, teachers, doctors, social workers, etc., to live in the area they serve. Everything must be done to build up indigenous leadership, but where it is impracticable to say "Look out from among you," the Church must be able to say, "I am among you as one — or as half a dozen — that minister."

Such ministers will be like the new-style missionaries of whom John Taylor writes:

Their location and their terms of service will be determined by [their secular] contracts: their relationship to the local church will be that of any layman seeking ways of missionary obedience in fellowship with other Christians in his place of work and neighbourhood.

And what he goes on to say applies, *mutatis mutandis,* just as much to the Church at home:

I no longer see a missionary society as primarily a recruiting agent for an overseas Church, nor as a means of getting people overseas who would not otherwise go, but as a fraternity of men and women each of whom is bound in a common commitment, specific and exacting enough to create a profound sense of membership among those who share it.

And yet to channel a single penny of the money fed into the dioceses through the Church Commissioners to such a housing association is legally impossible. It is all tied up to benefices and salaries and the provision of churches. And it is so compartmentalized that one cannot use benefice income for curate's housing or money from pulling down a church for building a hall. Can the Church of England possibly be flexible enough for the ministry of the future?

The hope lies in the fact that none of this makes sense except ecumenically. Certainly the Methodists will not tolerate what Anglicans have learned to put up with — as God forbid that we should be saddled with their (self-imposed) rule book. So while talks towards unity go on at the top, let us see to it locally that the shells are so broken that the eggs cannot be unscrambled.

CHAPTER 22
LOCAL LITURGY

Whatever the merits of the draft Order for Holy Communion produced by the Liturgical Commission of the Church of England — and they are real — it leaves the language basically untouched. It may get us out of the seventeenth century but it does not get us into the twentieth. It suspends us in fact in an artificial liturgical world of its own, unrelated to space or time, in which nobody really lives. The same is true of the comparable liturgy for Africa, which is fine but has nothing distinctively African about it at all.

Perhaps — but only perhaps — this is inevitable when a liturgy is being written for a whole country, let alone a whole continent. Probably it is also inevitable for anything that has to get a two-thirds majority in Convocation and Church Assembly. But even here, with the English church scene changing as rapidly as I believe it now is, I suspect that any report or commission is likely to find itself overtaken by events. The attempt to do a Revised Standard Version, as opposed to a New English Bible, on any aspect of the Church's life — though unavoidable in the first instance for softening up — will, I

believe, in the not-so-long run prove hopelessly conservative.

Meanwhile, let us grant that for the statutory services
it is necessary to start from the old language and the old
cadences. At the same time I hope we shall recognize the
urgency — before the top blows in any case — of beginning also where people actually are today. By that I mean
with liturgy which is *not* for all time and all places,
which is never intended for any vote in Convocation, but
which expresses the real needs of local Christian groups
— often *ad hoc,* frequently functional rather than geo-
graphical, and increasingly ecumenical. I believe that at
this point we should see genuinely free experiment, subject, as far as possible, to the bishop's *jus liturgicum.* For
otherwise there will be much spilled and divisive effort
that will not be channeled into discovering what we
really want at the more formal level.

The trouble is that this is very demanding and calls
for more than local skills. Most services or prayers that
attempt to start from life fall headlong into one or both
of two pitfalls. Either the wording is intolerably verbose
and does not stand up to corporate repetition. Or it is
purely ephemeral, with no dimension either of the ages
or of eternity.

On a recent visit to the United States I came across a
liturgy that I believe succeeds in avoiding both of these
traps. I found myself sharing in it at the Urban Training
Center in Chicago, where it fitted completely naturally.
But it was written for St. Mark's-in-the-Bouwerie, New
York — Damon Runyon country, in the notorious Lower
East Side of the city.

The genesis of the liturgy, which is printed at the end
of this chapter, is I believe significant for the way in

which these things ought to be fashioned. It was described to me in a letter from the Rector, Michael Allen, who was before ordination a senior editor of *Look* magazine:

Bishop Corrigan of the National Church approached me in the fall of '64 and asked if we could attempt an ecumenical and contemporary eucharist for student use.

I gathered together a group of people from the parish, a couple of older women, the curate, a priest member of the congregation, and a number of young people — college students and recent graduates, including one very good poet. We began meeting every other Tuesday night in the parish hall for discussion and communion.

Since none of us knew very much, we decided to celebrate according to Taizé, Church of South India, and Boone Porter's reworking of the Hippolytan rite. Each time we experimented with ceremonial and discussed the general direction of what we were doing, and began to feel out what the Holy Communion is all about.

After some weeks we agreed on a general format, i.e., what to keep in, and in what order, and what to leave out.

Then we assigned various people various jobs. The confession in its original form was written by a twenty-three-year-old girl, quite artistic, quite lovely. The original draft of the consecration was written by a twenty-five-year-old man — curiously enough a deeply troubled young man going from crisis to crisis in his own life. And so on.

Then the months went by and each evening we tried different forms, different renditions, always celebrating according to what we had written so far. This I think was absolutely essential because finally it was our experience of the worship itself which validated or did not validate what we were doing. Finally last fall we had several expanded meetings with Bishop Corrigan involved, and a local Presbyterian minister who is chairman of the Presbyterian Liturgical Commission, and we arrived at the present form.

During the progress of this I did most of the editing myself and occasional rewrites which were then redone by the group itself. And I wrote the dismissal. So you see this was very much a common project, and it finally involved W. H. Auden, who is also a member of this parish. I took it over to him and we spent an afternoon on stylistic matters — no fundamental rewrite, but the reworking of various phrases. The little phrase "for we are very deaf" is Auden's.

At this point I suggest that the reader break off to read the liturgy, which speaks for itself.

From its opening "We are here" to its inspired treatment of the final *ite, missa est,* it has the simplicity of form that follows function. It takes up the best of the traditional, and has the power and economy of the old Roman rite. Apart from the Scripture passages and the free intercession, it says all that needs to be said in 468 words, of which no less than 382 are monosyllables. It also has a refreshing directness. The people intervene themselves, instead of having their prayers prayed for them.

The strength of the liturgy may be judged by contrasting the climax of its thanksgiving with the corresponding portion of the Liturgical Commission's draft:

Wherefore, O Lord, having in remembrance his saving passion, his resurrection from the dead, and his glorious ascension into heaven, and looking for the coming of his kingdom, we offer unto thee this bread and this cup; and we pray thee to accept this our duty and service, and grant that we may so eat and drink these holy things in the presence of thy divine majesty, that we may be filled with thy grace and heavenly blessing.
Through the same Christ our Lord, by whom, and with whom, and in whom, in the unity of the Holy Spirit, all honour and glory be unto thee, O Father almighty, from

the whole company of earth and heaven, throughout all ages, world without end. Amen.

This latter, from its "remembrance [of] his saving passion" through "the presence of thy divine majesty" to its inflated doxology, transports us into a world of liturgical absenteeism. Its substitution of "heavenly blessing" for "heavenly benediction" is a good example of what I would call an RSVism — as, for instance, in the RSV's "intercedes [for "maketh intercession"] for the saints according to the will of God" in Romans 8:27, compared with the NEB's "pleads for God's own people in God's own way."

Those who made the St. Mark's liturgy would be the last to say that it could not be improved. It has not really tackled what I am sure cannot be put off much longer in liturgy or hymnody, namely, a serious attempt to reckon with the questions Bultmann has raised in theology. "O Father, who sent your only son into the world to . . . walk among us, as a man, on our earth" still makes Jesus sound like a being from another planet who was, astonishingly, really human. How to rewrite this would be an interesting subject for competition — for those who feel the difficulty. Those who do not, need not enter.

But I hope that this will not distract from the central issue I want to raise here. Any community needs for its health local as well as national newspapers and broadcasting. And it was a sad day in the history of the Church when local liturgy finally got absorbed. It is no criticism of the St. Mark's eucharist that it could not simply be taken over as it stands and used anywhere. I doubt, for instance, whether its confession transplants altogether easily from the world of the ghetto which shaped it. It is essentially local liturgy. But I hope it may serve as a point of departure for similar exploration, stimulated and guided by those with wider resources and authority.

The Eucharistic Liturgy

As prepared by the People and Clergy of St. Mark's-in-the-Bouwerie, New York, for use on special Ecumenical Occasions.

THE PREPARATION

At the appointed time, when all the people have assembled, the bishop, as president of the assembly, or some presbyter appointed to stand in his place, facing the assembly, shall say:

PRESIDENT: We are here.

ASSEMBLY: In the name of Jesus Christ.

PRESIDENT and ASSEMBLY: We are here because we are men — but we deny our humanity. We are stubborn fools and liars to ourselves. We do not love others. We war against life. We hurt each other. We are sorry for it and know we are sick from it. We seek new life.

PRESIDENT: Giver of life, heal us and free us to be men.

PRESIDENT and ASSEMBLY: Holy Spirit, speak to us. Help us to listen for we are very deaf. Come, fill this moment.

Silence for a time.

THE SERVICE OF THE WORD

Old Testament Lesson.

Psalm (*Said responsively*).

Epistle (*Read from the same place and in like manner to Old Testament lesson*).

Hymn.

The Gospel (*Read in the midst of the assembly, all the people facing the reader*).

Sermon.

Intercessions (*The deacon shall bid the prayers and intercessions of the assembly. He may lead them in a litany or with free prayers*).

THE OFFERTORY

The president shall begin the offertory with the following words:

If you are offering your gift at the altar, and there remember that your brother has something against you, leave your gift at the altar and go; first be reconciled to your brother, and then come and offer your gift. (Matt. 5:23).

After which he will turn to the deacon first and then the reader saying:

Peace, my friend.

And the deacon will answer:

Peace.

Then the deacon and reader will give the "Peace" to representatives of the congregation gathered before the altar table, and they in turn will pass it to all the people, while others will collect the alms.

Then the president shall read the following words:

I appeal to you therefore, brethren, by the mercies of God, to present your bodies as a living sacrifice, holy and acceptable to God, which is your spiritual worship. Do not be conformed to this world, but be transformed by the renewal of your mind, that you may prove what is the will of God, what is good and acceptable and perfect (Rom. 12:1–2).

Then shall be sung a hymn, during which time represen-
tatives of the people will bring the money along with
bread, water, and wine, and place them on the holy table.
The deacon shall prepare the bread and wine.

THE ACT OF THANKSGIVING

PRESIDENT: Lift up your hearts.

ASSEMBLY: We lift them to the Lord.

PRESIDENT: Let us give thanks for God's glory.

ASSEMBLY: We give thanks, we rejoice in the glory of all creation.

PRESIDENT: All glory be to you, O Father, who sent your only Son into the world to be a man, born of a woman's womb, to die for us on a cross that was made by us.

ASSEMBLY: He came for us. Help us to accept his coming.

PRESIDENT: He walked among us, a man, on our earth, in our world of conflict, and commanded us to remember his death, his death which gives us life; and to wait for him until he comes again in glory.

ASSEMBLY: We remember his death; we live by his presence; we wait for his coming.

PRESIDENT: On the night he was betrayed, the Lord Jesus took bread (*here he should lift up the bread in thanksgiving*); he gave thanks; he broke it, and gave it to his disciples, saying, "Take, eat, this is my body. Do this in remembrance of me." He also took the cup (*and here he should lift up the wine*); he gave thanks; and gave it to them, saying, "Drink of it, all of you; this is my blood of the covenant, which is poured out for many for the forgiveness of sins."

ASSEMBLY: Come, Lord Jesus, come.

PRESIDENT: Therefore, remembering his death, believing

in his rising from the grave, longing to recognize his presence; now, in this place, we obey his command; we offer bread and wine, we offer ourselves, to be used.

ASSEMBLY: Everything is yours, O Lord; we return the gift which first you gave us.

PRESIDENT: Accept it, Father. Send down the spirit of life and power, glory and love, upon these people, upon this bread and wine (*here he may extend his hands over the bread and wine*), that to us they may be his body and his blood.

ASSEMBLY: Come, risen Lord, live in us that we may live in you.

PRESIDENT: Now with all men who ever were, and will be, with all creation in all time, with joy we sing (*or,* say):

PRESIDENT and ASSEMBLY: Holy, holy, holy, Lord God Almighty, all space and all time show forth your glory now and always. Amen.

PRESIDENT: And now, in his words, we are bold to say: The Lord's Prayer.

Then shall the president break the bread before the assembly saying:

PRESIDENT: The gifts of God for the people of God.

ASSEMBLY: Amen.

THE COMMUNION

Then shall the president and other ministers receive Holy Communion into their hands, and then distribute the bread and wine to all present.

For the bread shall be said:

PRESIDENT: The Body of Christ.

ASSEMBLY: Amen.

For the wine shall be said:

PRESIDENT: The Blood of Christ.

ASSEMBLY: Amen.

When all have communicated, the president and other ministers shall gather the fragments and consume them. During this time the assembly may sing a hymn.

THE DISMISSAL

PRESIDENT: Go. Serve the Lord. You are free.

ASSEMBLY: Amen.

CHAPTER 23
POP PRAYER

The previous chapter was on liturgy that begins from life, locally, where it is lived. This is concerned with nonliturgical worship that starts from the same source.

It will consist in the main of reporting, followed by some reflections and questions. I shall concentrate on personal spirituality rather than public services. But, at the latter level, I have the impression that there is a considerable amount of creative ferment, particularly among young people, which is throwing up new and dynamic forms. One such, called "Be Yourself," was sent to me recently from the youth group at St. Andrew's, Edgware. Another, the school leavers' service in the Borough of Greenwich, was pointed and controversial enough to hit the headlines. I hope that someone is gathering up the experience gained through such experimentation. Otherwise, as in the title of a book of prayers[1] (not very good) of the type discussed later, it will be so much "spilled milk."

But in passing I would mention two collections that

---

1 Kay Smallzried, *Spilled Milk: Litanies for Living* (Oxford University Press, New York, 1964).

have been published. The first, *Modern Psalms by Boys*,[2] was compiled by Raymond Hearn from teaching in a London comprehensive school. The other is *New Hymns for a New Day,* which makes up a recent number of *Risk*,[3] the journal of the Youth Department of the World Council of Churches. The introduction by its secretary, Albert van den Heuvel, is a pungent answer to those who wonder why anything new is necessary.

But now I turn to the area of more personal devotion — though the old, improper distinction between *private* prayer and corporate worship is, like so much else, dissolving. The material I have come across — and I stress how haphazard this is — divides itself mainly into French-speaking Catholic and American-speaking Protestant.

Of the former, the classic is, of course, Michael Quoist's *Prayers of Life*. One says of course — but it is a book that has established itself so silently that many still may not know it. It appeared in the original as long ago as 1954, and when I first saw it I thought it so French as to be untranslatable. But it has been brilliantly rendered by two women, one French and one English, and published in Ireland.[4] I missed any reviews of it, and its fame has spread largely by word of mouth.

It starts from life just as it comes — the Telephone, a Five Pound Note, the Pornographic Magazine, a Bald Head — and turns it all not only into prayer but often into poetry as well. (The Sea is not only pure poetry but an example, not so common in this genre, of equal sensitivity to nature as to that which "wears man's smudge and shares man's smell".) It is almost uniformly quotable.

[2] University of London Press (London, 1966).
[3] II, 3, 1966.
[4] M. H. Gill, Dublin, 1963.

Lord, Why Did You Tell Me to Love? happens to be the first I dipped into, and it remains unforgettable.

Also from the French are *Prayers from the Ark* by Carmen Bernos de Gasztold, translated by Rumer Godden,[5] a Thurberesque *Beast in Me* type of devotion, delightful rather than profound. Then there is the work of Louis Evely, the Belgian priest, director of the Cardinal Mercier College and Chaplain to the Charles de Foucauld Fraternities. His retreat meditations, *That Man Is You* (with a preface by Congar),[6] were recommended to me in America as belonging to the same type as Quoist. I don't think they do. They do not so much start from life. But they certainly relate to it.

It is the native American products that suggest the title Pop Prayer. First among these one must place Malcolm Boyd's collection, with its squirm-making title, *Are You Running with Me, Jesus?*[7] This is Quoist in prose, prayer in the raw, with the last varnish gone. "All human life is there," as *The News of the World* would say, in all its warmth and all its lovelessness, laid bare before God. Malcolm Boyd, formerly in advertising, is an Episcopalian priest whose ministry has lain in state universities and civil rights. Section headings indicate the scope of this very worldly holiness: Prayers in the City, Meditations on Films, Prayers for Sexual Freedom, and so on. What he calls in his introduction "the heretical gap" between the holy and profane has quite disappeared.

It was a fellow Episcopalian priest, Robert Castle, who wrote the Litany for the Ghetto, which caused a furore when it was used in 1965 by the Chicago Negro

5 Macmillan, London, 1963.
6 Newman Press, Westminster, Maryland, 1965.
7 Holt, Rinehart and Winston, New York, 1965.

minister, Archie Hargeaves, at the biennial convention of the United Church of Christ. Indignant letters followed in *The Christian Century* for weeks afterward. Here there is such an identification between God and the city that grammar is strained to breaking point in bringing together the "Thou" addressed and third-person indicative of those who *are* the city:

O God, who lives in tenements, who goes to segregated schools, who is beaten in precincts, who is unemployed . . .
Help us to know you
O God, who is cold in the slums of winter, whose playmates are rats — four-legged ones who live with you and two-legged ones who imprison you . . .
Help us to touch you

and so on, ever nearer the bone.

Finally, I should like to commend Robert A. Raines' *Creative Brooding*.[8] He is a Methodist who has done a notable job in more traditional parish ministry, first in Cleveland and now in downtown Philadelphia. His book is a collection of daily readings, each starting with an excerpt from some contemporary writer or journalist and leading into carefully chosen Biblical passages and some very direct prayer. It uses the secular to "sharpen thought and provoke reflection."

If one were to try to sum up the marks of this mode — or should one say, mood — of prayer, certain things recur. Its controlling rubric might be Dag Hammerskjöld's "in our era, the road to holiness necessarily passes through the world of action."[9] Indeed, its key preposition is

[8] Macmillan, New York, 1966.
[9] *Markings* (Knopf, New York, 1964), p. 108.

"through." God is to be met in, with, and under, not apart from, response to the world, the neighbor. Its entry to God, the *ens realissimum,* is whatever *is* most real, however irreligious. Its form of the divine is more often than not the Son of Man incognito, whose presence is to be known obliquely, parabolically, brokenly — but always presently. Its style is that of a secular mysticism, with each of these words equally stressed. There is — in Christ — no gulf, no difference even, between ordinary life and prayer. And, needless to say, any special holy language or devotional diction is out. The Thees and the Thous have gone without trace.

And yet is it saturated with awareness of the world as "Thou" — and with the meeting through it of "the eternal Thou." As an art form it is liberally interspersed with vocatives — usually "Lord"; in Boyd, as often as not, "Jesus." The Deity is invoked freely, not to say chummily. It reads like devotional *Don Camillo,* with "the Lord" always around, as a gnome on the shoulder or a friend at the side.

And this conversational tone is odd, because Malcolm Boyd says specifically that he has come to see prayer as "not so much talking to God" [10] as "just sharing his presence." It appears often much more like Jesus sharing Boyd's presence and being conveniently at hand to compare notes with. But even at its best, as in Quoist, there is the sense of talking to a third person, apart from and invisible to the person whose concern engages one. Does this take the "Thou" of the other with real seriousness and the fact that the claim of the unconditional must be

[10] In his subsequent, and excellent, book of "secular meditations," *Free to Live, Free to Die* (Holt, Rinehart and Winston, New York, 1967), the vocatives have disappeared completely.

met *in him* and *through him* — even if it is not possible or natural to say "Lord, Lord"?

Is there a relic here of the Telstar image of prayer, of redirecting messages off a celestial being? Has this been replaced — instead of demythologized — by a three-cornered conversation? The current pop prayer idiom, with its stage asides, strikes me in fact as less truly incarnational than the (far more reserved) Quaker tradition of spirituality, which has its ambience much more *in* the Spirit and sees the Presence rather in terms of that which lights up every man from within, or, as Buber would put it, is *"between* man and man."

The strength of this contemporary prayer style is that it is inescapably personal. It knows God as given in response to the whole of life as Thou. Its weakness is that it is often artificially personalistic — envisaging God as a separate Thou. Is "O Lord" the last remnant of the poetic diction of a bygone age — or is it unavoidable? And if so can we use rather than stumble at the myth?

The Litany for the Ghetto with its identification of God with the scene rather than the spectator here seems to me to have the advantage. It has provoked the inevitable charge of pantheism. But it is not asserting a metaphysical identity between God and man; simply that at the given moment for the subject in prayer this is where, and who, God is — and there is no turning aside, not even to Another. So I find myself returning, in spirituality, to the fully personal panentheism, characteristic in this field also of Eastern Orthodoxy and Teilhard de Chardin, of the "God dwelling incognito" at the heart of all things.

CHAPTER 24
IN
SUM

I am often aware as I speak and answer questions that the real, unexpressed, elusive question is this: "What is this man really after? What makes him tick? What is at the back of what he writes and says?" At the risk of some repetition and even more omission, let me try to say as simply as possible what my deepest concern is.

One of the reviews of *Honest to God* ended with these words: "The book is fundamentally not an essay in unorthodox theology, but a venture in evangelism." That I accept. My fundamental passion is a missionary one. But it is mission with a difference.

Traditionally mission has been concerned with the heathen. But at no point is there a greater contrast between what I have called the old Reformation and the new.

For Martin Luther, the missionary task of the Church was in principle complete: there were no nations to whom the Gospel had not been preached. And in the 1662 Book of Common Prayer there are only two references to the non-Christian world — to the "Jews, Turks, Infidels and Hereticks," for whom we beg "mercy" on

Good Friday, and to the "natives in our plantations," for whom, says the Preface, the newly introduced adult baptism service "may be always useful."

Then there was mission virtually nowhere. Now there is mission virtually everywhere — and that, not merely in the sense that Christians are everywhere surrounded by nonbelievers, but in the sense that there is no presentation of the Gospel, if only to ourselves, which does not presuppose a missionary situation.

Let me illustrate this from what to this generation, and surely to every generation, lies at the heart of the Christian concern and debate — the word God and the reality for which it stands.

In the past, the missionary proclamation of the Christian Church presupposed that this was something at the center of our lives which we had to convey to the heathen on the remoter borders of civilization. But today it is not the heathen who are remote but the word God itself. For most people, if God comes in at all, it is on the edges of their everyday experience, after all the vital connections have been made, over and above them rather than in and through them.

It was this that lay behind my purpose in questioning the images of a God "up there" or "out there." There is, of course, absolutely nothing wrong with these images if they make God real for men, as they have done in the past and undoubtedly do for many still. But today their effect for millions is to locate God in an area of experience in which they no longer live with any vital part of their being.

In other words, he has ceased by definition to be God. He is no longer the *ens realissimum*, the most real thing in the world. Indeed, to introduce God is for most people

— and, let's admit it, for many younger Christians — to bring in what is often most remote from their deepest concerns, most problematic for them, most peripheral to what really makes them tick.

Does God-talk really *add* anything at all? That is the question we are all being forced to ask. *That* is why all proclamation today is in some sense missionary proclamation. We have to begin by convincing and convicting ourselves.

In this situation what do we do? The way in, I am persuaded, is from what I have called "the other end" [1] — that is, not from the words, the doctrines, the definitions, which seem so distant, but from whatever *is* most real for people. It is an inductive approach, like that to all knowledge in the modern world. Men need to be convinced that theology, like other sciences, is a genuinely open-ended search for the truth, in which the results are not prescribed. There is no word calculated to set up so much resistance as "dogma" — though it comes simply from the word used in Acts 15 when the body of Christians first said: "It *seemed good* to the Holy Spirit and to us." The Church felt its way, inductively, to certain conclusions and definitions; and it is these that it has offered to men in its preaching.

But today there is a limit to the possibility of starting from the answers at the end of the book. People simply do not understand "given" truths, and if we merely confront them with these in doctrine or in morals and say "Take it or leave it," then in most cases they will leave it. They require to work out the sum for themselves. They say, like St. Thomas, "Unless I see in his hands the

1 See my book *The New Reformation?* (Westminster Press, Philadelphia, 1965), especially Chapter 2.

print of the nails, and place my finger in the mark of the nails, and place my hand in his side, I will not believe."

To begin here is not to prescribe the ends negatively any more than positively. In fact, St. Thomas came through to the most complete expression of faith in the New Testament: "My Lord and my God." But it is to insist that the way through is *from* experience *to* authority, from relationships to revelation, from immanence to transcendence, rather than the other way round.

And this is a profoundly Biblical approach to truth. The Prophets were constantly insisting that the way to the knowledge of God was through obedience, sensitivity, justice, in the events and relationships of everyday life. And when the modern young person says that the only thing that is authoritative for him is what authenticates *itself* as real, valid, true, meaningful, he is not far from the conception of authority Jesus was trying to communicate to the Pharisees in John 10: "My sheep *know* my voice."

So if we are hoping to make God real for ourselves or for anyone else, we must start with whatever *is* most real for them, with whatever *matters most*. This will, of course, vary with the individual concerned. But there are, I believe, certain things from which we can start that are shared by many of our generation, however split and mixed up it may be.

Let me list six, very summarily:

1. There is the very real sense of *integrity* felt by the artist and by the scientist and indeed by the technologist (with his honesty to the medium, etc.) — which one cannot betray without "selling out."

2. There is the passionate sense of *justice* which comes out in the Freedom Movement and the race issue

and underlies the current wave of indignation about Vietnam, as group after group rises up and asks one to join in protest.

3. Connected with this last is the very real sense of *solidarity* with the sin and suffering of our fellowmen. A recent letter I had on Vietnam asked me if I would join a group to fly out to Hanoi to be bombed — to say, in effect, to the Americans: "If you go on bombing the city, you bomb us with it." Whether one agrees with this politically or not, or, if one does, whether it is the most efficacious method, one cannot help recognizing here something of the identification of the suffering servant.

4. Part of this, again, is the inescapable sense of *responsibility*, of being one's brother's keeper, which makes anything but some form of welfare state and poverty program a moral impossibility today. "The great society" and the implications of our involvement in "one world" will not let us go.

5. There is the concern that underlies so much of this that *persons matter* as persons for their own sake. This is the implicit theology behind what has been called "the faith of the counselors," which recognizes that in the end it is caring love that alone makes men whole.

6. There is the closely connected sensitivity to *quality of relationship* as the real test of morality, rather than some external rule — that things are right, for instance, if they are inside marriage but wrong if they are outside, right if they are heterosexual but wrong if they are homosexual, and so on. The criterion of what makes for deep, stable, mature, free personal relationships seems to so many of our gen-

eration, both Christians and others, the more significant test.

These are all judgments that cut deep and take us a long way. The difference between "I-Thou" and "I-It" is meaningful to a generation for whom the classical distinctions between time and eternity, God and the world, are almost meaningless. And this I believe is an important way into theology — that is, to the understanding of ultimate reality as personal. It is the way of the Incarnation — through the stable door of an ordinary human experience and ordinary human relationships.

And I am sure that we have to be able to show Christ *in the first instance* as the definition and vindication of a completely human existence: "Behold the man." That was where the disciples had to start; and *from that* they went on to see him also as the clue to all existence, the one in whom, as St. Paul put it, all things cohere and hang together. In him they saw a window through to the final reality of God at work, so that they were compelled to confess that "God was in Christ reconciling the world to himself" and to recognize the claim of Jesus' whole life that "he who has seen me has seen the Father."

But this generation goes on to ask, with the men in the parable of the sheep and the goats, "But, Lord, when did we see you?" Bonhoeffer's question "Who is Christ for us today?" cannot be evaded. In the messianic, hieratic clothing of so much Christian proclamation and art men's eyes are kept from recognizing him. In this post-Christian age he must once again be enabled to come alongside men, as he came alongside the disciples on the Emmaus road, in the first instance as the gracious neighbor, the man for others, *before* he can make himself known as the Messiah of whom their Scriptures speak.

Christ remains for the Christian absolutely central. "Jesus is Lord": that is the earliest Christian creed and the distinctive feature of the Christian Gospel. And I have no desire whatsoever to change or dilute it. Indeed, I am content to say with St. Paul: "I determined to know nothing among you save Jesus Christ and him crucified." In other words, with Herbert Butterfield: "Hold to Christ and for the rest be totally uncommitted." Be free to admit that you are a Christian agnostic, that is a *Christian* who does not *know* a great deal. "On the borders," said Bonhoeffer again, "it seems to me better to hold our peace." The center for the Christian is firm: the edges and the ends are gloriously and liberatingly open.

INDEX

31, 32, 57–60, 66, 67, 75, 107;
Second Coming of, 61–64; *see
also* Virgin Birth doctrine
John, St., 101, 107
John the Baptist, St., 126
Jung, Carl Gustav, 128
Jus liturgicum, 144

Kant, Immanuel, 86
King, Martin Luther, 104
Koinonia, 114

Laplace, Pierre Simon de, 86
Lay ministry, 131–35, 137–41
Lewis, C. S., 106
Litany for the Ghetto, 155, 158
Liturgical Commission, Church
of England, 143
Liturgy, 143–51
"Living Stream, The," 128
Logos, 18
Luke, St., 107
Luther, Martin, 159

Markings, 156n
Marx, Karl, 87
Mary, Mother of Jesus, 43
Ministry, *see* Clergy
Miracles, 49–52
Mission of the Church, 141, 159,
161
Modern Psalms by Boys, 154
Murry, John Middleton, 108

Napoleon Bonaparte, 86
National Church, 145
Nature, laws of, 13
New Blackfriars, 140
New Christian, 123, 129
New English Bible, 53, 143
New Hymns for a New Day, 154
"New Morality," 77–81
New Reformation?, The, 161n
New Testament, 31, 33, 37, 44,
49, 50, 59–60, 61, 62, 63, 66, **75,**
100, 102, 105, 107, 109, 112,
114, 132, 162
New Theology, 33, 73–76
Newton, Isaac, 86
Nietzsche, Friedrich, 23
Nihilism, 23

Old Testament, 38, 44, 66, 101,
114, 132
Ordination, 131–34, 136–41

Pantheism, 92–93, 158
Parables, 50, 62
Patmore, Coventry, 99
Paul, St., 59, 68, 103, 111, 126,
128, 164, 165
Pentecost, 108, 118
Peter, St., 50–51
Phenomenon of Man, 128
Phillips, J. B., 106
Porter, Boone, 145
Prayer, 153–57
Prayers from the Ark, 155
Prayers of Life, 154
Presbyterian Liturgical Commis-
sion, 145
Priesthood, 132, 134, 140; *see
also* Clergy
"Priesthood and Paternalism,"
140
Profumo, John, 78
Prophets, 49, 90, 114, 162

Quoist, Michael, 154, 155, 157

Raines, Robert A., 156
Renaissance, religious art in, 124
Resurrection doctrine, 30, 31, 32,
57–60, 66, 67, 75, 107, 108
Risk, 154
Romantic movement, religious
art in, 124
Room at the Top, 78

About the Author

John A. T. Robinson is a rare combination of first-rank New Testament scholar, efficient administrator concerned with the reorganization of the Church of England, and Bishop with a deep insight into the needs and problems of ordinary people. Long before the success of *Honest to God* made his name a household word throughout the English-speaking world and beyond, he was known for his controversial views on morality and on the need for theology to be really "applied" so that it had relevance to the concerns of the modern world.

Born into a clerical family in 1919, he was educated at Marlborough and at Cambridge. Immediately after the end of World War II, he was a curate in Bristol, later going to Wells Theological College as chaplain. From 1951 until he became Bishop of Woolwich in 1959, he was Dean of Clare College, Cambridge, and he has lectured frequently in the United States.

In addition to his work as a Bishop, he continues to write learned articles on New Testament subjects as well as books and articles on the problems of Christian belief today, to lecture abroad, and to broadcast on radio and television. He is married and has four children.

About the Editor

Ruth Nanda Anshen, philosopher and editor, plans and edits Perspectives in Humanism, World Perspectives, Religious Perspectives, Credo Perspectives, and The Science of Culture Series. She writes and lectures on the unity of knowledge in relation to the unity of man.